Roelien Immelman holds a degree in Information Design from the University of Pretoria. Her first major position was in London, where she illustrated for Michiko Koshino, a prominent Japanese fashion brand. After a brief stint as layout designer for a Cape Town-based publisher, a hankering after the unknown first led her to the Far East, and she has been freelancing and exploring the world ever since. She has worked as illustrator for various publications and clients all over the world, but the projects that stand out are those in which she could combine drawing with her other great passions: food and travel. Always armed with sketchbook, pens and ink, as well as her unique point of view and keen eye for detail, Roelien has explored, cooked and illustrated her way through the culinary landscapes of Europe and Southeast and East Asia. Personal highlights include cooking beef rendang in Penang, drawing recipes for coconut curries in Sri Lanka, learning to cook delicious bûn cha in Vietnam, making peanut salads under moringa trees in Myanmar and cooking dashi from scratch in Japan. Her work has been exhibited in South Africa and Taiwan. Another recent example of her distinctive style of food illustration is to be found in *Tuistafel* by well-known South African home cook, Errieda du Toit. Roelien shares a mountain house in Taipei with her ceramic artist husband, De Waal Immelman, their baby Miems, and Bleep the cat.

Follow her on instagram
@unrouxly or unrouxly.co.za

For my granddaughters, Isabella and Sophie

Michael

For my father,

who taught me how to draw and who loved his food.

How pleased he would be knowing I combined the two.

Roelien

Bertie Booysen
1932–2013

Published in 2021 by Penguin Books
an imprint of Penguin Random House South Africa (Pty) Ltd
Company Reg. No. 1953/000441/07
The Estuaries, 4 Oxbow Crescent, Century Avenue, Century City, 7441
P O Box 1144, Cape Town, 8000, South Africa

www.penguinrandomhouse.co.za

Publisher: Beverley Dodd

Managing editor: Cecilia Barfield

Editor and indexer: Joy Nel

Principal designer: Helen Henn

Illustrator and designer: Roelien Immelman

illustration

Photographers: Mike Robinson and Athabile Mpofu

Food stylist: Brita du Plessis

Food stylist assistants: Kate Ferreira and Thandi Mammacos

Proofreader: Bronwen Maynier

ISBN 978-1-48590-087-0

Reproduction by Hirt & Carter Cape (Pty) Ltd
Printed and bound by C and C Offset Printing

Contents

Acknowledgements

A big and special 'Thank you' to my wife, Madeleine, for her support and counsel and comment.

Also, to Roelien, my partner in this book, my illustrative designer, you have made this book the most amazing work of art. Thanks to De Waal and Miems for giving you the time to work your magic.

To Sophia Lindop. What an inspiration you are, and friends you and Paddy have been. Your enthusiasm for what we do is beyond compare.

To Mike Robinson for his photography, lovely to have worked with you after a gap of 30 years. To Brita du Plessis, food stylist, you have made the food come alive.

To the team at Penguin Random House, Beverley Dodd, publisher, and Helen Henn, designer. Two new friends who took on this project with great enthusiasm.

To Joy Nel, my editor. How fabulous it has been being bossed about by and working with you again. Your freshness, fabulous food knowledge and way with words is eclectic and worthy of unconfined praise.

To my English language guru, Bruce Jack, winemaker of note, for always being willing to help with the use of words and names.

Now, in no particular order, my love and thanks to:

Petrina and Rob Visser of Dalewood Fromage, an Appellation Controlée Paarl Cheese Estate. Thank you for your (and your ladies') sensational cheese. How wonderful it has been working with your utterly sublime produce. Of the best cheese in the country.

My friend of 40 years, Ina Paarman. A mentor, a teacher, the Queen of the South African Kitchen with her brilliant products.

Peels Honey, for the finest honey ever, all the way from KwaZulu-Natal.

Brenda and Nick Wilkinson of Rio Largo Olive Oil, you anointed us with your superb quality products. Brilliant to have a truly fine oil with which to work.

Paul and Tracy of NOMU. Our food is seasoned each day by your rubs, seasonings and other products, and the love you put into them.

Michael Fridjhon and Michael Crossley of Reciprocal Wines, suppliers of fine wine and spirits to the author. And your wonderful Riedel glassware for my wine tastings. Can I ever go back to pressed glass again?

And, finally, to Sharon and Lauren, of Oregano, the finest pâtisserie in Linden. Your bakes, your love and friendship have eased the passage of this book.

And if I have left you out, know that you are loved...

Roelien says: Michael, for your gentle energy and infinite knowledge. What a privilege to work with you. A big thanks to De Waal, who made the most tea in his life, and for all his support and input. And to my friend Jani, who provided a lifeline for Miems and I, I couldn't have done it without you.

A few words about prickly pears...

I grew up on my parents' wine farm in Durbanville. It was a typical Cape wine farm – a large Cape Dutch-styled house with lovely teak windows and doors, built in the early 1900s. It had a pair of gables in the front from which cascaded deep blue wisteria plumes in season. It had a large stoep that was regularly polished with Cobra Red polish and a large General Electric floor polisher that had two large brushes. In summer, as it faced east, it was a lovely place to have afternoon tea, a ritual in our lives.

My parents had a loved lady, called Maggie, who lived with us, the widow of my father's farm manager. Maggie was a superb cook and a great baker. She made great use of the fruits that were typical of a Cape farmyard at the time – Cape gooseberries, figs, mulberries, a quince hedge, loquats, pomegranates, rough-skinned lemons, a youngberry fence...

Late afternoon, when the day had cooled down, Maggie would appear from the nether regions of the kitchen with a broom and a *visblik*, her trusty rusty Lucky Star pilchards tin, which lived between seasons in a treasured place in the kitchen to make sure it was there for next year's prickly pears. She would bear down on the prickly pear cactus, which stood at the bottom of the garden like a collection of large green dinner plates all piled one upon the other, the edges of which were lined with prickly pears. Maggie had a knack for choosing pears at the point of perfect ripeness. She would put the *visblik* over one and snap it off. These freshly picked ones would be lined up on the lawn until such time as she

had enough. She would then pick up her broom and sweep the prickly pears up to the front door, by which time they had lost all their prickles.

This was but the beginning of the process. The prickly pears overnighted in the fridge to firm up and make them easy to peel. They were peeled by being topped and tailed, then a slit made down the side and then, using a small knife, Maggie worked her way round to cut the skin away. The prickly pears were then placed in a white enamelware dish and covered with kitchen paper and a purpose-crocheted cotton doily with cowrie shells around the edges to weigh the paper down.

And then, the sheer deliciousness of eating them. When prickly pears were in season, there was always a plate of them in the large kitchen fridge with the heavy door for us to eat when we got home from school. More pip than flesh, but it was the coolness that made them so attractive after walking up the drive in a heat that had crows sitting open-mouthed in the trees and cicadas screaming so loudly as to deafen you.

Sliced, at times with ice cream, sometimes with our farm cream. Most often, taken in hand from the fridge and eaten over the cement outdoor washing sink off the kitchen to let the juice, which ran down our chins, not go onto our clothes...

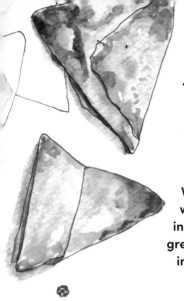

Buffet ~ Old Cape Style

In November 2000, I was asked to present a Cape Table, buffet style, for lunch on Voyager Estate for the Margaret River Wine Festival in Australia. The recipes are all well known. What Madeleine and I did was to pull each recipe apart, change or add ingredients, modernise the cooking methods and add flavour. The wine festival was a great success, with many former South Africans coming down from Perth. Many of them in tears when they saw the food... These are the recipes we devised for the occasion.

Voorgeregte / First Courses

Hoofgeregte / Main Courses

Groente / Vegetables

Nageregte / Desserts

Koffie (Coffee)

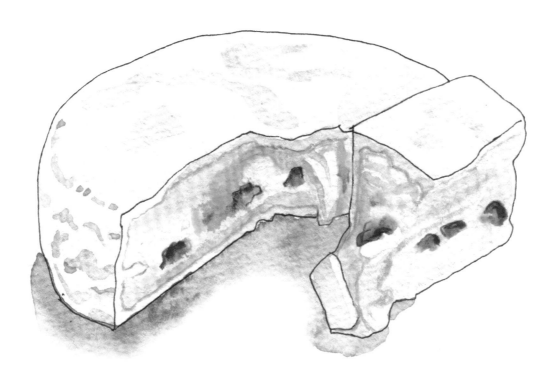

Starters, Salads and Light Meals

So often starters can be used as light meals, and small light meal portions as starters. They are meant to rouse your appetite ahead of the meal, so the portion size should be small in anticipation of the main course. Often a wine that you have had as an aperitif will be a great partner to the starter. And then a switch to another wine more appropriate for the main course.

Boontjiesop

Old-fashioned Hot Bean Soup

Cass Abrahams – Cape Malay cuisine authority – says in her book *The Culture and Cuisine of the Cape Malays*, '... there isn't a great variety of soups in the Cape Malay Cuisine ... the same basic recipe is used and is named after the thickening agent: peas, beans or lentils.' This soup could originally have been brought to the Cape by settlers from Holland, for whom the early Malay settlers cooked in their homes.

VEGETARIAN VERSION

375 g dried sugar beans

Water for soaking

45 ml sunflower oil

3 large onions, chopped

2 large leeks, plus a bit of the green tops, chopped

3 carrots, peeled and thickly sliced

3 turnips, peeled and thickly sliced

200 ml skinned and chopped ripe tomatoes, drained

1.5 litres extra water

Sea salt and freshly milled black pepper

A knife point of ground cloves

A knife point of cayenne pepper

A knife point of grated nutmeg

A knife point of ground allspice

2.5 ml ground mace

Grated rind of 1 lemon (no pith)

Chopped fresh parsley for sprinkling

1 small chilli, seeded and finely chopped

MEAT VERSION

1 kg beef shin or marrow bones

125 g pork fat or bacon, chopped

The day before, pick over the beans and eliminate any bad ones, then soak overnight in cold water.

The following day, drain and discard the water.

In a heavy-bottomed saucepan, gently heat the oil and, when hot, fry the onions, leeks, carrots and turnips until soft and lightly browned. Be careful not to burn any of the vegetables. Remove from the oil and set on kitchen paper to drain.

If using meat in the soup, gently fry in the oil (adding more if necessary) until lightly browned. Remove and set on kitchen paper to drain.

Place the beans in the saucepan, add the onion mixture, tomatoes and meat (if being used) and pour over the 1.5 litres water. Season lightly with salt, freshly milled black pepper, cloves, cayenne pepper, nutmeg, allspice and mace. Bring to the boil, then lower the heat and simmer for 1½–2 hours until the beans are soft. Remove any scum or foam from the top during the simmering.

Remove the beef or marrow bones (if using), and cut up the meat into small pieces. Discard the bones.

Using a potato masher, mash the vegetables. Or remove some of the vegetables to give some texture to the soup and blitz the remaining soup in a food processor. Stir the meat and whole vegetables back into the soup.

Taste the soup for seasoning, adding more salt and pepper if required. Add the lemon rind, parsley and chilli and return to the stove to heat through thoroughly. Check for final seasoning and serve in hot bowls with buttered slices of wholewheat bread.

Serves 6

 A chilled medium cream Spanish Sherry

Komkommersop

Cold Cucumber and Potato Soup

**Cucumber mixed with mint and yoghurt is often used as a cooling sambal when served with curry.
This is a cooling soup, which is ideal served before a curry as a first course, or as a light meal or lunch.**

3 large cucumbers, peeled and seeded

Sea salt and freshly milled black pepper

A little sunflower oil

2 large onions, finely chopped

3 large potatoes, peeled and diced

500 ml chicken or vegetable stock

15 ml chopped fresh mint leaves

15 ml chopped fresh flat-leaf parsley

1 small bunch spring onions, well washed
 and finely chopped

1 small sweet pickled gherkin, finely
 chopped

250 ml milk

90 ml thick plain yoghurt

50 raw almonds, roasted and
 finely chopped

Grate the cucumbers coarsely, place in a colander and sprinkle lightly with salt. Allow to stand and drain for 30 minutes. Press out the liquid and set on kitchen paper to drain.

Heat the oil in a saucepan and gently sweat the onions until soft but not coloured. Add the potatoes, grated cucumbers and stock. Season with salt and pepper. Bring to the boil, reduce the heat and simmer until the potatoes are cooked through.

Blitz the soup in a food processor until smooth, then pour back into the saucepan and add the herbs, spring onions and gherkin, reserving a little of each for garnish. Add the milk and reseason if necessary. Allow to cool and then chill in the refrigerator.

Serve the soup in chilled bowls, garnished with the reserved spring onions, gherkin, parsley and mint, a tablespoonful of yoghurt and a sprinkling of roasted almonds.

Serves 6

 A delicate white wine, Colombard

Samoosas

Vegetarian Version

After bobotie, samoosas are one of the best-known Cape dishes, thought to have originated in India. The best ones I have ever eaten were on the Grand Parade in the city of Cape Town. As a boy, I used to buy them while waiting for a bus to take me from school to the suburbs. They could at times contain beef, chicken or a curried vegetable mix, as given here. Although available throughout the year, they are especially used on the morning of the Eid al-Fitr feast at the end of the holy month of Ramadan. The dough used is usually homemade and called pur.

60 ml vegetable oil

2 cm-thick slice fresh ginger, very finely chopped

1 red chilli, finely chopped

6 spring onions, sliced (keep green and white parts separate)

1 large onion, chopped

2 cloves garlic, finely chopped

5 ml curry powder or garam masala (see p. 171)

2.5 ml turmeric

2.5 ml ground coriander

1 ml ground ginger

120 g potatoes, peeled and diced

120 g carrots, peeled and diced

Tomato purée, to moisten if necessary

100 g young spinach leaves, cooked

Juice of ½ lemon

1 small bunch fresh coriander leaves, finely chopped

6 sheets phyllo (for baking) or spring roll pastry (for deep-frying)

1 free-range egg, beaten

Heat the oil in a pan and fry the ginger, chilli and the white parts of the spring onions, the onion and the garlic, stirring continuously, until they begin to colour. Add the spices and cook for a short while to release the aromatic oils. Add the diced potatoes and carrots, and tomato purée if necessary. Continue to cook, stirring from time to time, until the moisture has almost evaporated and the mixture is cooked through.

Stir in the spinach, the green parts of the spring onions, the lemon juice and the coriander leaves. Cover the pan, remove from the heat and set aside.

Cut each phyllo or spring roll sheet in half lengthwise. Fold both long sides of each piece of pastry over to the centre to make a narrow strip about 5 cm wide with two strengthening 'hems'.

Place two teaspoons of the vegetable mixture at the top of a strip of pastry. Fold one corner over to make a triangle shape at the top, then turn the triangle over at the base, and continue to fold in the same way until you reach the end of the pastry strip and have a fat triangle-shaped samoosa. Brush the inside of the last fold of pastry with a little beaten egg and seal the samoosa. Repeat with the other pastry strips and the rest of the filling. Place the samoosas on a baking tray and set aside.

If using phyllo pastry, preheat the oven to 180 °C. Bake the samoosas for 25–30 minutes or until puffed and golden brown. If using spring roll pastry, you will have to deep-fry them in hot oil.

The samoosas can be served immediately or allowed to cool and eaten later as a snack.

Serves 6

As this is a Muslim dish of origin, I would suggest a good tonic water

Snoekpatee

Snoek Pâté

Snoek is a firm game fish that is served in many different ways. When I was a boy, I remember fishermen on horse-drawn carts blowing tin fish horns to announce their presence in my grandmother's street. Kalk Bay Harbour during a snoek run is a popular place to buy fresh fish. If you are lucky, the fisherman will fillet the fish for you. Curried snoek-head soup is a very popular dish, accompanied by much sucking of bones! Snoek pâté is served in many restaurants and coffee shops around Cape Town.

250 g smoked snoek (any firm fleshed fish, such as angelfish, can be used instead)

150 ml sour cream

125 g soft butter

Grated rind and juice of 1 lemon

Freshly milled black pepper

4 spring onions, green part included, well washed and chopped

15 ml chopped capers

30 ml finely chopped fresh parsley

Shred the snoek between your fingers and place it in the bowl of a food processor.

Add the sour cream, butter, lemon rind and juice. Season with freshly milled black pepper. Process until smooth.

Stir in the spring onions, capers and parsley. Taste for seasoning and add more lemon juice (or white wine vinegar) or black pepper if required.

The pâté can be packed into a ramekin and covered in melted butter, or simply placed on a plate. It is usually served with either Melba toast or wholewheat seed loaf and butter. In the winelands of the Cape, it is served with whole Muscat grape jam (*korreltjiekonfyt*) in a limpid syrup.

Serves 6

Unwooded Chardonnay

Fattoush

Fattoush is a Middle Eastern and North African salad using toasted pita bread. It's a delicious salad option from the other tip of Africa.

2 pita breads, cut into 1 cm dice

½ cucumber, halved lengthwise, seeded and cut into small chunks

2 medium tomatoes, skinned

½ red onion, thinly sliced

1 red pepper, thinly sliced

1 small handful each fresh mint, parsley and sweet basil leaves, washed and picked into small pieces, stalks finely chopped

DRESSING

5 ml cumin seeds, toasted

2.5 ml ground sumac

5 ml sea salt

Freshly milled black pepper

2.5 ml palm or light brown sugar

30 ml extra virgin olive oil

30 ml lemon juice or red wine vinegar

Preheat the oven to 180 °C.

Place the pita bread pieces on a baking tray and toast in the oven until very crispy.

Place all the dressing ingredients into a small bowl and whisk until combined.

Toss all the salad ingredients together in a bowl, add the dressing and mix quickly. Check and adjust seasoning. Allow to stand for 15 minutes – no longer as you need to keep the pita pieces crisp – before serving.

Serves 2

 A fresh, crisp Blanc de Noir

Panzanella

Panzanella is an Italian bread and tomato salad which is usually served with a roast or chicken or fish dish. It's a great way to use up stale bread. I have demonstrated this at the African Relish cookery school in Prince Albert to the delight of the students.

45 ml extra virgin olive oil

200 g stale ciabatta, cut into thumb-size pieces

Sea salt

1 English cucumber, peeled

1 jar roasted red peppers, sliced

600 g baby tomatoes, halved

1 small red onion, halved and thinly sliced

2 wheels Dalewood Fromage feta cheese, broken up (three if you use other brands)

1 small handful each capers and pitted Kalamata olives

Your favourite salad dressing

Freshly milled black pepper

Sweet basil leaves for garnishing

Mixed salad greens for serving

Heat the olive oil in a large frying pan. Add the bread and sprinkle with sea salt, and fry over low to medium heat until nicely browned.

Halve the cucumber lengthwise and use a teaspoon to remove the seeds. Cut into thin slices and place in a large salad bowl. Add the roasted red peppers, tomatoes and red onion. Add the feta, capers and olives. Fold in the bread and toss through the salad dressing. Taste and season with more sea salt and freshly milled black pepper. Cover and leave at room temperature for at least 30 minutes.

Garnish with basil leaves and serve on a pile of mixed greens.

Serves 6

 Dry Viognier

COOK'S NOTE

To jazz it up a bit, you can add 8 chopped anchovy fillets.

The Bacon, Lettuce, Camembert and Tomato Salad Sandwich

This is a BLT with a college education. I love the Camembert from Dalewood Fromage, so creamy and soft. The milk used for their cheese is from a pasture-reared Jersey herd.

250 g rindless streaky bacon

60 ml good-quality mayonnaise (not the tangy kind)
(see also p. 170)

10 ml Dijon mustard

1 short-length baguette

100 g mixed salad leaves

2 large ripe tomatoes, skinned and sliced

Sea salt and freshly milled black pepper

1 ripe Dalewood Fromage Winelands Camembert, sliced

Kettle-fried potato crisps for serving

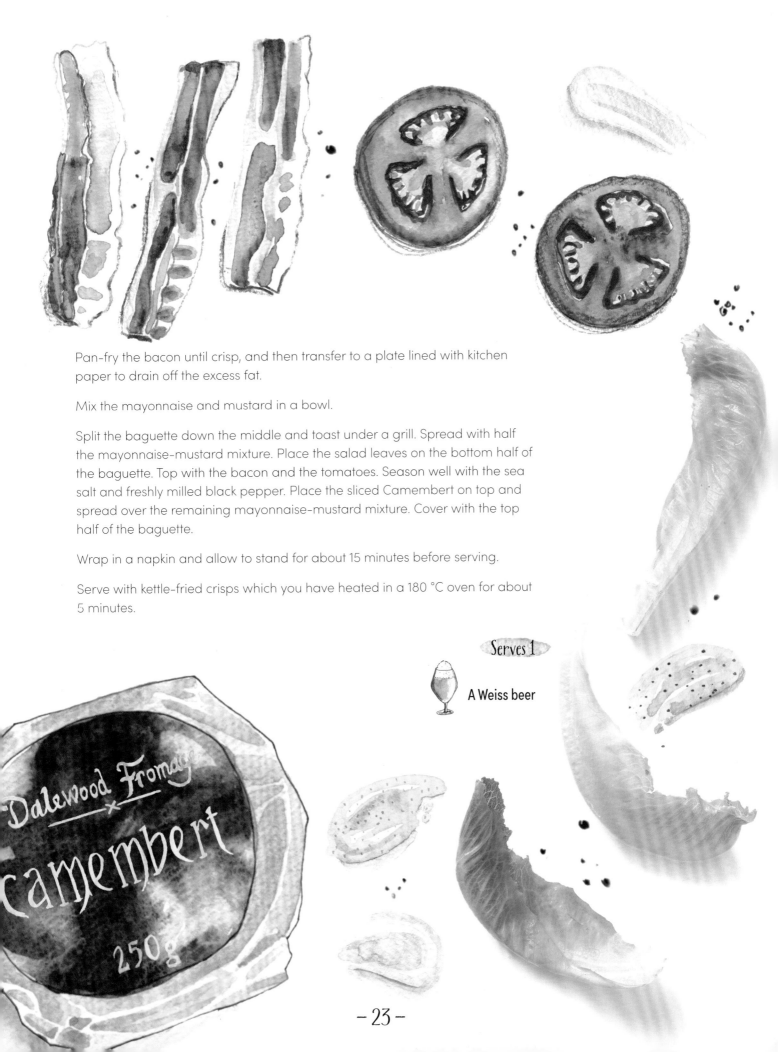

Pan-fry the bacon until crisp, and then transfer to a plate lined with kitchen paper to drain off the excess fat.

Mix the mayonnaise and mustard in a bowl.

Split the baguette down the middle and toast under a grill. Spread with half the mayonnaise-mustard mixture. Place the salad leaves on the bottom half of the baguette. Top with the bacon and the tomatoes. Season well with the sea salt and freshly milled black pepper. Place the sliced Camembert on top and spread over the remaining mayonnaise-mustard mixture. Cover with the top half of the baguette.

Wrap in a napkin and allow to stand for about 15 minutes before serving.

Serve with kettle-fried crisps which you have heated in a 180 °C oven for about 5 minutes.

Serves 1

A Weiss beer

Dalewood Fromage
×
Camembert

250g

The Ultimate Cheese and Tomato Sandwich

This is not the sort of recipe that requires accurate amounts, but The Ultimate Cheese and Tomato Sandwich has minimum requirements.

Fry some finely chopped onion slowly in butter until caramelised, then set aside to cool to room temperature.

Have ready an excellent bread knife – it'll do for the bread and the tomato.

You'll need fresh soft white bread. Could be a baguette, a ciabatta or focaccia.

Tomatoes are important: vine-ripened in the sun to the point of perfection, plump and firm for easy slicing.

The cheese? Dalewood Fromage Huguenot aged for a year. If you want a softer flavoured cheese, try the Dalewood Fromage Boland. It has the flavour elements of a mild Cheddar – you want the tomato to shine through.

For the construction, cut two slices of bread in medium to thick slices and spread with soft butter.

Thinly spread over some of the caramelised onion.

Slice the tomatoes thinly and layer generously over the onion. Season well with sea salt and freshly milled black pepper.

Top with torn sweet basil leaves and pile on the grated cheese. Top with the other slice of bread.

Slice on the diagonal and serve with fresh rocket dressed with verjuice and olive oil of the extra virgin kind.

A treat we have on occasion when we have a braai is to make up the sandwich and tie it in a little parcel with some sewing cotton, and when the coals are cooling, lightly toast the sandwich on both sides. This will cause the cheese to melt slightly and ooze out the sides. Yum! (These are known as *braaibroodjies*.)

Serves 1

A full-bodied Rosé

Dolmades

Stuffed Vine Leaves

We lived in a house with two enormous grape vines in rural Bergvliet. I made this dish from young fresh unsprayed vine leaves picked from the vines in our garden. If you leave it too late into early summer, the leaves become woody. A traditional Greek dish called dolmades, it is often served cold as mezze. Dolmades are also delicious served hot with an egg and lemon sauce.

Pick about 35 vine leaves for this recipe and trim the stalks right onto the leaf. Soak for a while in heavily salted water to get rid of any bugs. Check for eggs on the back of the leaves and remove them. Roll the leaves up like a cigar in bundles of about six leaves and tie with a piece of string. Simmer for 5 minutes in boiling salted water. Lift out with a pair of tongs, turn them on end and allow to drain. Set aside to cool.

35 fresh young vine leaves, about the size of your hand, prepared as described above, plus enough to cover the dolmades in the casserole

Extra virgin olive oil

250 g cleaned chicken livers, cut into about three pieces each

Sea salt and freshly milled black pepper

100 g pistachio nuts or almonds, roughly chopped

Grated rind of 1 lemon

10 g chopped fresh parsley

10 fresh mint leaves, finely sliced

1 large onion, finely chopped

3 cloves garlic, finely chopped

A good pinch of dried chilli flakes

200 g uncooked long-grain rice

375 ml chicken stock

Juice of 2 lemons

EGG AND LEMON SAUCE

4 free-range eggs

125 ml lemon juice

5 ml cornflour (optional)

330 ml hot chicken stock

Sea salt and freshly milled black pepper

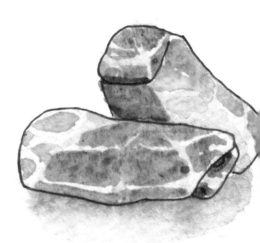

In an enamelled cast-iron casserole, flood the base with a thin layer of oil. Heat over gentle heat. Quickly stir-fry the chicken livers to brown on the outside, but leave pink on the inside. Remove the chicken livers, season well, add the nuts, lemon rind, parsley and mint and set aside.

Wipe out the casserole with a piece of kitchen paper and add 15 ml or so oil and heat thoroughly. When hot, add the onion and stir-fry until starting to colour. Add the garlic and continue frying for a minute or so. Be careful not to burn the garlic. Add the chilli flakes and the rice and fry for a short while so that the rice heats up and absorbs some oil. Add the chicken stock, lemon juice and chicken liver mixture and bring to the boil. Lower the heat, cover with a lid and cook gently until the rice is almost cooked and still has a little 'bite'. Remove from the heat and allow to cool.

Preheat the oven to 180 °C. Splash a little olive oil into a baking dish and line with a few leaves, shiny side up.

Lay out the remaining vine leaves on a table, shiny side down. Divide the rice mixture amongst them. Roll up from the stem side, tucking in the sides as you go so that you end up with a nice little parcel. Pack them neatly into the dish and top with more open vine leaves. Cover with baking paper and bake at 180 °C for 30 minutes.

While the vine leaves are baking, make the sauce. Beat the eggs in a saucepan, then whisk in the lemon juice and cornflour. (If you are confident that you can make the sauce without it curdling, leave out the cornflour.) Continue whisking while you pour in the hot stock. Cook the sauce over very low heat until it thickens and the cornflour tastes cooked. Season well and keep warm until you are ready to serve.

Serve the dolmades warm with the egg and lemon sauce.

Serves 8–10 as a first course or use it as part of a buffet

Assyrtiko if you can find one, or a Riesling

Oeufs en Meurette

Eggs in Red Wine

**This is an easy-to-prepare recipe. It's a Burgundian dish,
so you need a good fruity Pinotage for the cooking.**

CROUTES

8 slices good-quality sourdough bread

Extra virgin olive oil

1 clove garlic, peeled

EGGS AND SAUCE

750 ml Pinotage (you can also use Pinot Noir,
Grenache Noir or Cinsault)

500 ml NOMU Beef Stock (prepared as per
packaging instructions)

8 jumbo free-range eggs

1 onion, thinly sliced

1 carrot, peeled and thinly sliced into penny shapes

1 stick celery, thinly sliced

1 clove garlic, finely chopped

2.5 ml black peppercorns

1 bunch fresh herbs (thyme, parsley stalks, and
a bay leaf)

Sea salt and freshly milled black pepper

GARNISH

30 g butter

8 small onions, peel and clean the root and then cut
into quarters through the root to keep them whole
(if you can get shallots, peel them, clean the root
and keep them whole)

180 g pancetta or bacon, cut into strips

180 g baby button mushrooms, trimmed and
quartered (leave whole if you buy the very small
ones; you can also use sliced oyster or other exotic
mushrooms)

Chopped fresh parsley

CROUTES

It's best to do this bit while you are simmering the sauce so that
the croutes are at room temperature when you serve them. Cut
the slices of sourdough into rounds with a large pastry cutter or use a
small saucer to guide you. Fry in a non-stick pan with a slick of extra virgin
olive oil. Salt lightly and drain on kitchen paper. Or bake dry in a 180 °C oven until crisp.

Rub the croutes with the garlic clove and set aside.

EGGS AND SAUCE

Bring the wine and beef stock to the boil in a wide saucepan. Turn
down to a gentle simmer. Carefully crack the eggs into the wine-
stock mixture and poach for 3–4 minutes until the yolks are just

set. Have ready a bowl of iced water to stop the cooking process. Carefully transfer the eggs from the wine-stock mixture into the iced water.

Now turn your attention back to the stock and wine. Add the onion, carrot, celery, garlic, peppercorns and bunch of herbs and simmer for 30 minutes. Strain off the vegetables, herbs and peppercorns, and continue simmering until you feel that you have a sauce on your hands.

In the meantime, prepare the garnish. In a frying pan, using butter, gently fry the onions or shallots for a while before adding the pancetta or bacon strips, and finally the mushrooms. Allow to cook through. Add to the sauce and simmer for 20 minutes in the saucepan.

You can thicken the sauce if you so wish with kneaded butter (*beurre manié*, a mix of equal parts flour and soft butter) and whisk in little peanut-size pieces of it until the sauce reaches your desired thickness. Check for seasoning and add sea salt and freshly milled black pepper.

Place the eggs into the sauce and allow them to heat through for a short while. Using a large soup plate, place a croute in the centre and carefully place an egg on top of it. Pour the sauce around the croute. Spoon some of the garnish around the croute and sprinkle with the parsley.

Serve with crunchy bread and a crisp, well-dressed green salad.

Serves 8 as a first course,
or 4 as a lunch or supper dish

Chilled Pinot Noir

Green Summer Minestrone

A different soup and a lighter, more delicate version of traditional minestrone. It's perfect for our hot summers or as a vegetarian option, and actually does very well as an iced soup too.

Extra virgin olive oil

1 large onion, thinly sliced

4 fat cloves garlic, crushed with coarse sea salt

1.5 litres hot vegetable stock

80 g frozen peas, defrosted in tap water

80 g asparagus spears, halved lengthwise

80 g fine French beans, halved crosswise

80 g baby spinach, weighed after trimming the stalks and cut into chiffonade

80 g long-stemmed broccoli, cut into strips

Sea salt and freshly milled black pepper

15 g fresh flat-leaf parsley, roughly chopped

15 g fresh oregano, roughly chopped

2 sprigs fresh mint, torn into shreds

Ciabatta cubes, toasted in the oven and cooled

Heat some olive oil in a large enamelled cast-iron casserole and stir-fry the onion for a couple of minutes until it becomes transparent. Add the garlic and cook for a short while. Add the stock, bring to the boil and then add all the vegetables. Simmer for about 5 minutes until the vegetables are cooked to your liking. Season with sea salt and freshly milled black pepper.

Dish up, sprinkle with the chopped herbs and a slick of olive oil, and serve with the ciabatta croutons.

Serves 6

A frisky young Chenin Blanc

Simple Curried Eggs

A huge favourite in our house, especially as a vegetarian option when our non-meat eating friends come to lunch. Usually served simply with steamed basmati rice, Mrs Ball's Peach Chutney (a real South African staple!), sliced banana and desiccated coconut. Some of us like it with a sambal of finely chopped ripe tomato and onion too.

8 extra-large free-range eggs

3 onions, thinly sliced (reserve one for garnishing)

2 fat cloves garlic, chopped

120 ml extra virgin olive oil

30 ml medium curry powder or garam masala (see p. 171)

1 tin (400 ml) coconut milk

½ tin (200 g) chopped peeled tomatoes (preferably Italian)

15 ml chutney

15 ml soft brown sugar

Juice of ½ lemon

Sea salt and freshly milled black pepper

50 g whole almonds, halved

50 g sultanas

Sprigs of fresh flat-leaf parsley

Steamed basmati rice for serving

Place the eggs in a saucepan and cover with water. Bring to the boil and simmer for 10 minutes. Pour off the hot water and immediately put the saucepan under cold running water (add a few blocks of ice) while cracking the shells. Leave the water dribbling through the saucepan until the eggs are quite cold. This will prevent the eggs from getting a blue edge to the yolks. Remove the shells and place the eggs in a bowl. Cover with cold water and set aside.

Fry the slices of two of the onions and the garlic very slowly in 60 ml of the olive oil until soft and golden in colour. Add the curry powder and fry for about 2 minutes. Stir in the coconut milk and tomatoes and bring to the boil. Reduce the heat and simmer for 10–12 minutes.

Add the chutney, brown sugar and lemon juice and season with sea salt and freshly milled black pepper.

In the meantime, fry the remaining onion in the remaining 60 ml olive oil until well browned and almost crisp. Remove carefully from the oil and drain on kitchen paper.

Fry the almonds in the same oil until light brown, and then follow with the sultanas (which will puff up), and briefly the parsley. Drain the almonds, sultanas and parsley on kitchen paper.

When ready to serve, heat the eggs in the sauce. Place the rice on a platter and spoon the eggs in the sauce down the centre. Garnish with the fried onions, almonds, sultanas and parsley.

Serves 4

 A tall glass of well-chilled Pale Ale

– 33 –

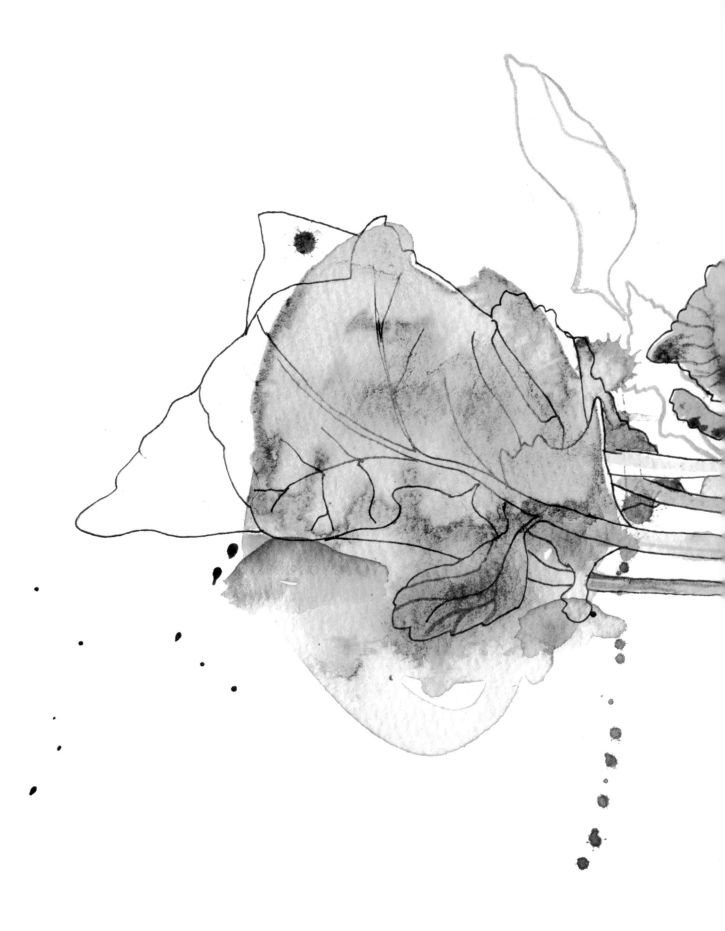

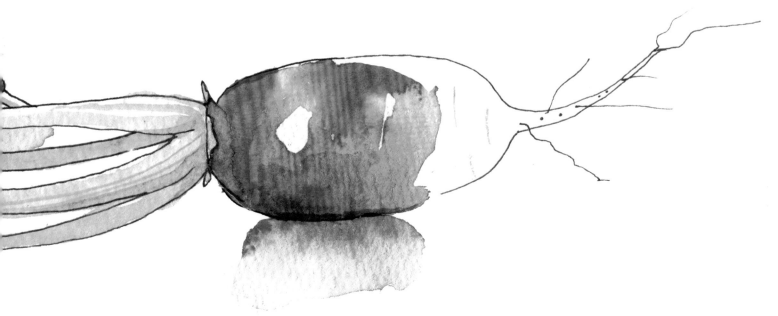

Vegetable Sides and Vegetarian Dishes

More and more of our friends are eating less meat and switching to plant-based dishes as main courses. These are featured here with some of the accompanying side dishes for my Cape Buffet (see p. 8). The Pumpkin Puffs are perfect with afternoon tea, or after supper when one plays games. Vegetarians need to be careful that they get their fill of protein, and vegans need to be sure to take supplements in order to get the full span of minerals and vitamins to keep them healthy.

Zucchini in Agrodolce

Sweet–Sour Baby Marrows

Agrodolce is a sweet-sour Sicilian way of presenting vegetables and sometimes fish. The flavours are loved by South Africans, who enjoy the sweet-and-sour combination.

500 g baby marrows

Fine sea salt

A little extra virgin olive oil

Freshly milled black pepper

A pinch of ground cinnamon

30 ml golden sultanas

30 ml toasted pine nuts

30 ml white wine vinegar

30 ml sugar

Slice and salt the baby marrows and allow them to drain for an hour. Rinse off and pat dry with kitchen paper.

In a saucepan with a lid, cook the baby marrows in the olive oil over low heat until nearly done.

Season with the freshly milled black pepper and cinnamon. Add the sultanas, pine nuts, white wine vinegar and sugar. Cook with the lid off until almost all the liquid has cooked away – there should be a small amount of syrupy sauce left.

Serve hot as a vegetable or cold as a salad.

Serves 4 as a side dish

Something white and crisp and fresh, or a glass of Vermouth over ice

Sweet-and-Sour Onions with Moskonfyt

This is my take on a dish I had once in the 1970s and have thought of ever since. I usually make it with small 'pickling' onions, but when I saw some shallots recently, I bought them and made this dish, using moskonfyt instead of the sugar used in the original recipe. (Moskonfyt is a grape juice syrup. You can also use pomegranate or agave syrup.) If you have fresh thyme, put in whole sprigs and remove the stalks at the end of cooking; the leaves usually come off during the cooking process. If you are not able to find shallots, pickling onions will do as well.

500 g shallots or pickling onions

70 ml extra virgin olive oil

15 ml tomato paste

125 ml white wine vinegar (or use red wine, apple cider or rice vinegar)

80 ml raisins or sultanas

7.5 ml dried thyme

30 ml finely chopped fresh parsley

1 fat clove garlic, finely chopped

250 ml boiling water

30 ml moskonfyt

Sea salt and freshly milled white pepper

Peel the shallots or onions, keeping the root end intact to prevent them from breaking apart. In a saucepan, brown the onions in the olive oil over gentle heat until they are well coloured all over. Take them out of the saucepan and set aside.

Remove the saucepan from the heat and add the tomato paste, vinegar, raisins or sultanas, herbs, garlic, water and moskonfyt. Stir well to dissolve the tomato paste and then bring the mixture to the boil.

Return the onions to the saucepan, turn down the heat to a simmer and cover with a lid. Simmer for about 50 minutes, adding more water as you go along if you feel it necessary. Once the onions are tender, remove the lid and cook over high heat to reduce the liquid until it forms a thick glaze.

Place in a covered dish or glass jar in the fridge and serve cold with cold meats or sausages over the next few days.

Serves 4 as a side dish

White, perhaps with a little residual sugar

Niël's Pumpkin Puffs

Niël Stemmet* and I have known each other for 30 years. He is so talented in terms of design, décor, hospitality and cooking. He uses Afrikaans as his medium, in an interestingly quirky way.

Niël says: 'My loved cook Emily made these puffs, which we served mainly with main courses, at Le Must Restaurant in Upington. Guests came from far and wide to eat these puffs. And, as they stand, they become more chewy and nicer. So, you can make them a little before the meal. You can also enjoy the puffs with custard or Greek-style yoghurt, then you can call them pudding.'

* Sadly, Niël died of COVID-19 just after sending me this recipe. A huge loss of a unique person.

750 g cooked and mashed pumpkin

2 free-range eggs

5 ml sea salt

500 ml self-raising flour

15 ml baking powder

500 ml sunflower oil

SYRUP

500 ml sugar

250 ml water

125 ml fresh cream or milk

30 ml butter

A pinch of sea salt and a knife point of white pepper

2.5 ml ground cinnamon

2.5 ml ground ginger

10 ml cornflour

Beat together the pumpkin, eggs and salt until creamy. Sift the flour and baking powder three times, then stir it well into the pumpkin mixture to form a soft dough. Heat the oil in a heavy-bottomed saucepan until it is at medium heat. Drop spoonfuls of the dough into the oil. Do small batches at a time as it makes it easier to turn over the puffs. When golden, remove from the oil and place onto kitchen paper to absorb as much oil as possible, and keep warm.

Now prepare the syrup. Bring all the ingredients, except the cornflour, to the boil in a saucepan. Mix the cornflour with a little water to make a thin paste that looks like buttermilk. Stir this into the syrup mixture and cook for a short while to cook the cornflour and thicken the sauce. Pour the warm syrup over the puffs and serve.

Niël says: 'Geniet die ou-se-dae se lekkerte.' (Enjoy the deliciousness of the olden days.)

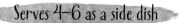

Serves 4–6 as a side dish

Pudding wine, a White Jerepigo perhaps? Well chilled ...

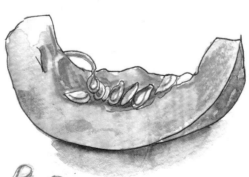

Geelrosyntjierys

Yellow Rice with Raisins

Yellow rice is known as *begrafnisrys* or funeral rice in the Cape, as it was traditionally served at large family gatherings such as funerals. Rice was either cooked as *droërys* (dry rice) or *paprys* (wet rice), though this one, as a type of pilaff, falls somewhere between the two. According to Cass Abrahams, the leading authority on Cape Muslim food, basmati rice is 'most prized' among the Cape Muslim community, though most homes use the ubiquitous American long-grain rice today. While saffron was used in earlier times, turmeric is the current favourite spice used for colouring the rice.

340 g basmati rice

125 g seedless raisins

100 g unsalted butter

1 onion, very finely chopped

1 whole clove garlic, peeled

1 piece stick cinnamon, about
    4 cm in length

2 cardamom pods, crushed
    to release the seeds

4 ml turmeric

Some threads of saffron

Sea salt

600 ml cold water

Sugar to taste

Place the rice in a bowl and pour over a kettle of boiling water. Stir for a while with a fork and leave to stand for 10 minutes. Pour into a sieve, drain and rinse under cold water.

Pour some boiling water over the raisins to plump them up.

Melt half the butter in a heavy-bottomed saucepan with a tight-fitting lid. Add the onion and the whole garlic clove and let them sweat gently until the onion is transparent. Add the cinnamon and cardamom pods.

Add the rice to the pan, turning it over several times so that each grain is covered in the hot butter. Add the turmeric, saffron, two very good pinches of salt and the cold water. Bring quickly to the boil, stirring only a little, and then reduce the heat to the lowest setting. Cover and cook for 11 minutes.

Remove the rice from the heat. Stir in the rest of the butter and gently fork it through the rice with the drained raisins and about 5 ml sugar (or more to taste). Cover and leave the rice to stand for 10 minutes. Remove the garlic clove before serving. I leave in the cinnamon, as it looks pretty in the rice when laid out on the table.

Serves 6 as a side dish

Pampoenkoekies

Pumpkin Fritters

Loved by children all over the country, pumpkin fritters can be rustled up at the last minute when unexpected guests arrive. If they are made with a well-ripened and dry pumpkin (or butternut squash) they are deliciously full flavoured and sweet. The fritters are traditionally served with wedges of the old Cape rough-skinned lemon, and castor sugar flavoured with ground cinnamon. They also freeze well for future use.

60 g cake flour

7.5 ml baking powder

A good pinch of sea salt

500 g pumpkin, peeled, steamed and finely mashed

2 free-range eggs, well beaten with a little milk and strained

Butter and oil for frying

Sift the flour, baking powder and salt together twice.

Place the pumpkin in a large bowl and beat in the flour mixture. Add the egg mixture and beat well. The batter should just keep its shape rather than run off the spoon. Add a little more milk if the batter is too stiff.

To cook the fritters, you can either heat a half-half mixture of butter and oil in a pan, or heat a griddle and line it with some buttered greaseproof paper. Place tablespoonsfuls of batter into the pan and fry gently until brown. Turn over and cook on the other side. Drain on kitchen paper and keep warm while you make the rest of the fritters.

Serve with lemon wedges and cinnamon sugar.

Serves 6 people with 4 fritters each

A cup of well-drawn Assam Tea

- 43 -

Slaphakskeentjies

Sweet-and-Sour Onions

Why this dish should be called 'weak heels' is lost in the mists of time, but it is a quintessential Cape dish on the South African table. The same sauce is sometimes used over freshly cooked young green beans.

24 small pickling onions or shallots

3 free-range eggs

45 ml white sugar

45 ml white grape vinegar

45 ml water

Grated rind of 1 lemon

5 ml yellow mustard powder

Sea salt and freshly milled black pepper

Chopped fresh parsley for garnishing

Place the onions in a large bowl and pour over boiling water. Allow to cool and then, when you are able to, slip the onions out of their skins, keeping them whole and the root intact. Use a sharp knife to clean up the root.

Boil the onions in lots of salted water until tender. Drain in a colander and set aside to cool in a salad bowl.

In the meantime, whisk the eggs well and pour into the top of a double boiler over gently simmering water. Add the sugar, vinegar, water, lemon rind and mustard powder and stir with a wooden spoon until the sugar has dissolved and the mixture has thickened like a custard. Remove from the heat and season to taste with salt and freshly milled black pepper.

Pour the hot sauce over the onions. Cover and allow to cool.

Garnish with chopped parsley before serving.

Serves 6 as a side dish

Sousboontjies

Stewed Sugar Beans

Sousboontjies **are a very popular dish in South Africa and usually put in an appearance on the Sunday lunch table, to be eaten with the Sunday roast! There are many recipes, each varying in quantities of vinegar and sugar used depending on the tastes of the household. For convenience, you can now even buy bottled** *sousboontjies* **off the supermarket shelves. This recipe will serve 6 as an accompaniment, but you can double up and keep some for a future meal as it keeps well in the refrigerator.**

250 g dried sugar beans or butter beans

Sea salt and freshly milled black pepper

100 ml white grape vinegar

100 g soft brown sugar

15 ml butter

Pick through the beans to ensure there are no bad ones, before weighing. Soak the beans in a bowl overnight, well covered with water so that the beans stay below the surface even after swelling.

Transfer the beans to a saucepan, cover with fresh water and bring to the boil. Reduce the heat and simmer very gently until the beans are cooked through and soft. Add a little more water during the process if necessary. When cooked, drain off any excess water and add salt to taste.

Take about 10 per cent of the beans and mash them with a potato masher. This will help to thicken the sauce.

Return the mashed beans to the saucepan with the vinegar, sugar and butter and simmer for a while to combine the flavours. More sugar and vinegar can be added at this stage to get the correct balance of sweet and sour for your personal taste.

Serve hot. (If serving cold, check for seasoning and add salt and pepper to taste.)

Serves 6 as a side dish

Soetpatats

Stewed Sweet Potatoes

Sweet potatoes are a very popular vegetable and are sometimes served whole in their skins with rich farm butter and salt and pepper. This recipe has them stewed in a sugary, honeyed, spicy butter and they're served this way as an accompaniment to bredies and roast meats. If you can get the yellow *borrie patats* variety of sweet potatoes and use yellow 'government' sugar (*goevermentsuiker*), so much the better.

1 kg sweet potatoes, peeled and thickly sliced

75 g yellow sugar mixed with a little ground cinnamon and ground ginger

100 g butter

Sea salt and freshly milled black pepper

3 strips orange rind, removed with a potato peeler and containing no pith

150 ml water

Preheat the oven to 180 °C.

In a heavy-bottomed casserole, layer the sweet potatoes with the sugar, butter, salt and freshly milled black pepper to taste and the orange rind. Pour the water down the side and bring to the boil on top of the stove. Cover with a tight-fitting lid and then bake in the oven for 45 minutes or until tender.

Bring back to the boil on the stovetop and reduce the liquid until it forms a glaze over the sweet potatoes.

Serves 6 as a side dish

Boereboontjies

Mashed Green Beans and Potatoes

**Traditionally, this dish has a piece of fatty rib of mutton cooked in the middle of the beans.
I offer a vegetarian version here. It was a favourite recipe of my mother-in-law, Anne Whittal.**

30 ml butter, plus extra

1 large onion, finely chopped

500 g fresh green beans, ends trimmed off, sliced

3 medium potatoes, peeled and sliced into thin rounds

Sea salt and freshly milled black pepper

250 ml water or vegetable stock

In a heavy-bottomed casserole, heat the butter, add the onion and fry gently until soft and translucent – do not brown.

Add the green beans and stir to coat with the onions. Add the potato slices and stir again.

Season well with salt and freshly milled black pepper and pour over the water or stock. Bring to the boil and then cover and simmer over gentle heat, adding more liquid if necessary, until the potatoes and beans are very soft and mashable.

Using a potato masher, mash the green beans and potatoes together. Taste and reseason if necessary, and stir in a knob of butter.

Serve hot with roast meat.

Serves 6 as a side dish

Risotto of Chicken of the Woods and Black Garlic

Foraging for fungi is a great hobby for those who live near forests. Chicken of the woods is a fungus which looks like layers of chicken meat. It has a good forest flavour with the texture of shredded chicken. Our friend Paddy Lindop brought us a lovely piece of fresh foraged chicken of the woods at the same time I was given some black garlic, so I put the two together.

60 ml extra virgin olive oil

1 onion, finely chopped

1 carrot, finely chopped

1 stick celery, finely chopped

300 g Arborio rice

250 ml dry white wine

4 cloves black garlic, finely chopped

1 litre chicken stock, heated to a simmer

400 g chicken of the woods (or oyster or porcini mushrooms), cut into small cubes

5 ml dried tarragon

Sea salt and freshly milled black pepper

100 ml fresh cream

100 g Parmigiano-Reggiano, Grana Padano or Pecorino, freshly grated, for serving

Heat the olive oil in a large, wide, deep pan. Add the onion, carrot and celery and cook until the onion starts turning golden. Add the rice and continue to stir for 1 minute. Pour in the wine and add the garlic. Allow the wine to almost boil away.

Ladle a little stock into the pan and stir well with a wooden spoon. As the stock is absorbed, add another ladleful at a time, stirring continuously. When you have added half the stock, add the chicken of the woods and the tarragon. When all the stock is absorbed – after 15–20 minutes – test the rice; it should have a creamy consistency. If the rice has a chalky thread through each grain, you will need to cook it for longer with a little more liquid. You can use hot water if you have no stock left.

When done, taste for seasoning and add sea salt and freshly milled black pepper and stir in the cream. Put a lid on the pan, remove from the heat and allow to stand for about 10 minutes. Serve sprinkled with the cheese.

Serves 4

A good, well-oaked Chardonnay

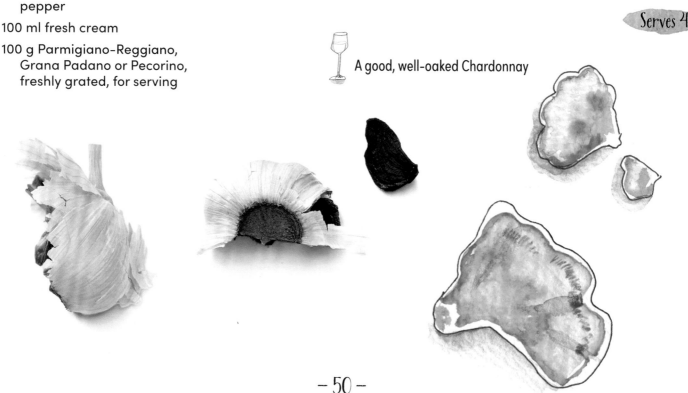

-50-

Usha Singh's Vegetable Biryani and Shredded Salad

I have only met Usha Singh twice, yet she feels like an old friend. I visit her website often and always find a recipe or a cooking tip and just know that her food is utterly delicious. Being a vegetarian, there are lots of exciting meat-free dishes on her website.

BIRYANI

375 g basmati rice

250 g brown lentils (tinned lentils can be used)

45 ml cooking oil

1 medium onion, chopped

2–3 pieces stick cinnamon

8–10 curry leaves

1 dried chilli

2 ml cumin seeds

2 ml mustard seeds

5 ml fennel seeds

10 ml ground ginger

10 ml chilli powder

5 ml ground cumin

5 ml ground coriander

5 ml turmeric

15 ml biryani ground mixed spices or garam masala (see p. 171)

8–10 baby potatoes, washed and halved

500 g frozen mixed vegetables of your choice

15 ml sea salt

10–15 ml cooking oil, heated

Chopped fresh coriander for garnishing

SHREDDED SALAD

150 g grated carrots

50 g thinly sliced yellow and red pepper

50 g grated radish (optional)

50 g finely sliced onions

100 g sliced cucumbers

100 g sliced mini rosa tomatoes

175 g finely shredded iceberg lettuce

DRESSING

25 ml finely chopped fresh mint

5 ml sea salt

35 ml apple cider vinegar

25 ml extra virgin olive oil

25 ml toasted sesame seeds

 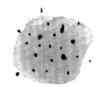

To make the biryani, soak the rice and lentils separately in warm water for about 15 minutes. (This step isn't necessary if you're using tinned lentils.)

Heat the oil in a large heavy-bottomed saucepan, add the onion and allow to brown over medium heat. Add all the spices and allow to cook for 1–2 minutes.

Add the soaked lentils, potatoes, mixed vegetables, rice, salt and about 250 ml water. Bring to a rapid boil, and allow to boil for 10–15 minutes.

Lower the heat and cook for another 35–45 minutes or until the potatoes are tender and the rice is cooked (add more water if necessary, but very little at a time).

If using tinned lentils, add them at the end, just to warm them through.

While the biryani is cooking, prepare the salad ingredients and place in a large mixing bowl. Toss after each addition.

Whisk or shake in a bottle all the dressing ingredients, except the sesame seeds, and pour over the salad. Toss lightly and sprinkle over the toasted sesame seeds just before serving.

Pour the heated oil over the biryani and garnish with chopped coriander before serving with the shredded salad.

Serves 4

 A glass of Gewürztraminer, spicy to meet spicy

Dalewood Wineland Wild Mushroom Brie Topped with Panko, Enoki Mushrooms, Thyme and Lemon Pangrattato

Petrina and Rob Visser make some sublime cheeses at Dalewood Fromage, where their Jersey herd feeds on grass pastures. Their renowned cheeses regularly win awards in local and international competitions.

Extra virgin olive oil

60 ml panko (Japanese rusk crumbs) or plain breadcrumbs

Sea salt and freshly milled black pepper

1 small handful enoki or shimeji mushrooms

250 g triangle Dalewood Fromage Wineland Wild Mushroom Brie (a plain Brie is also fine to use), at room temperature

Grated rind of 1 lemon

A few sprigs fresh thyme, picked

Preheat the oven to 180 °C. Make sure the shelf is in the middle of the oven. Pour a little slick of olive oil into a cheese baker or suitable small baking dish, and use a pastry brush to coat the inside.

Brown the crumbs in a small non-stick frying pan, season with salt and pepper and spread out to cool.

Fry the mushrooms in a little olive oil in a separate non-stick frying pan, then season with salt and pepper.

Place the cheese into the prepared dish and brush with a little olive oil. Place on a baking tray and bake in the oven for 12 minutes. The cheese should be bubbling when it comes out of the oven.

Mix together the crumbs, mushrooms, lemon rind and thyme leaves. Sprinkle generously over the baked cheese and serve with chunks of baguette.

Serves 2 as a main course or 4 as a post-dinner cheese

 A delicate red, Grenache Noir or Pinot Noir

Mira Weiner's Vegan French Toast

Mira lives in McGregor in the Robertson Wine Appellation, where she is involved in wine marketing for the many fine wineries in the valley. Lately, she has taken to producing some fine foods which are gluten, egg, dairy and refined sugar free. Bright, amusing and clever, she is the real deal and knows her stuff.

This recipe is a great breakfast or brunch option.

FRENCH TOAST

250 ml plant-based milk (I used almond)

15 ml chia seeds, ground

2.5 ml vanilla extract

4 slices rustic gluten-free bread (the drier the bread the better)

QUICK CHOCOLATE SPREAD (OPTIONAL)

45 ml natural almond butter – no sugar added (you can use hazelnut, macadamia, cashew or peanut butter too)

45 ml raw cacao powder

30 ml pure maple syrup

45 ml plant-based milk (I used almond, but oat or another nut milk would work well too)

TOPPING SUGGESTIONS

Ground spices such as ginger, cinnamon or nutmeg for sprinkling (optional)

Sliced bananas

Berry compote

Cinnamon whipped coconut cream

Raw cacao nibs

Rose petals

Gomasio sprinkle (toasted sesame seeds ground with pink Himalayan salt)

If using, make the chocolate spread first.

On a very low heat, whisk all the ingredients together for a few minutes. The sauce mustn't bubble or burn. Immediately remove from the heat once it is well mixed. If you prefer the sauce to be sweeter, add more maple syrup. If it's too thick, thin out with more milk.

Once cooled, it can be stored in a glass jar in the refrigerator for a few days (bring to room temperature or warm over low heat if it is very thick when you want to use it).

To make the French toast, whisk together the milk, ground chia seeds and vanilla extract. Refrigerate for 10–15 minutes. Take out of the refrigerator and whisk again.

Dip the bread slices into the mixture for a few seconds on each side. You don't want the bread to get so soggy that it falls apart, but each slice must be nicely coated with the mixture.

Heat a non-stick pan over medium heat and fry the bread slices for a few minutes on each side or until golden.

Serve with a generous smear of chocolate spread (if using) and your choice of toppings.

Serves 2

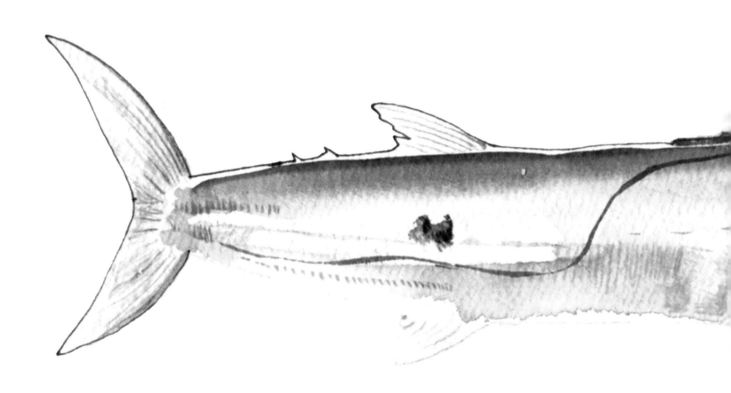

Fish

Many people are loath to cook fish at home and
prefer eating it in restaurants or other people's
homes. Get over this – fish is such a great protein and
if the cooking smell bothers you, open the windows.
There is a lovely selection of dishes in this chapter.
The ubiquitous Pickled Fish, almost a national dish,
is served especially at Easter when the weather is
usually warm though autumnal.

Braaied Yellowtail with Bo-Kaap Spices

There's nothing like a firm piece of game fish off the braai. Lucky for us, fresh fish is something you can lay your hands on anywhere in the country. Monkfish, yellowtail or swordfish are good ones to use. Make sure your fire is really hot.

4 large slices middle-cut yellowtail, skin on

Lemon juice for sprinkling

Sea salt

1 small onion, thinly sliced

2 fat cloves garlic, crushed with sea salt

1 thumb-size piece fresh ginger, peeled and grated

1 mild green or red chilli, seeded and thinly sliced

5 ml garam masala (see p. 171), or more if you want a bit more heat

Oil for brushing

Make some thin diagonal slashes on both sides of the fish portions. Sprinkle with lemon juice and sea salt and allow to marinate for about 30 minutes.

In the bowl of a small blender, place all the remaining ingredients, except the oil, and blend until almost smooth. Place in a dish large enough to marinate the fish. Add the fish and coat it well with the marinade. Allow to rest for 15 minutes.

When you cook the fish over the coals, lightly brush it with oil and cook it skin-side down first – this will hold the fish together. Once on the grill you will see that the flesh of the yellowtail turns opaque from the bottom up. It will take 4–5 minutes for the skin to crisp up. Using a fish slice or broad spatula, carefully turn the fish over and cook it for a further 3–4 minutes on the other side. Check the inside and it should be just cooked, with the flesh all turned just opaque. It will cook further once you have taken it off the braai.

Serve the fish, skin-side up, accompanied by a bowl of cucumber raita (a mix of grated cucumber and thick plain yoghurt with chopped mint).

Serves 4

A lightly oaked Chenin Blanc

Mark Dodson's Smoked Haddock Risotto with Wholegrain Mustard Sauce

In 1990, I was fortunate to work at the famous Waterside Inn at Bray-on-Thames. Michel Roux was running the restaurant at the time. It was a great experience working with Head Chef Mark Dodson – he taught me so much and was part of the success of our Restaurant Parks in Constantia. Mark and his wife, Sarah, own the very successful Masons Arms in Knowstone, Devon. Mark is also a member of Great British Chefs.

WHOLEGRAIN MUSTARD SAUCE

125 ml double cream

25 g wholegrain mustard

Sea salt and freshly milled
  black pepper

RISOTTO

15 ml extra virgin olive oil

50 g onion, finely chopped

175 g Arborio rice

100 ml white wine

600 ml fish stock

HADDOCK

200 g smoked haddock, skinned
  and pin-boned

150 ml double cream

50 g Parmesan, grated

POACHED EGGS

Water for poaching

Dash of white wine vinegar

4 free-range eggs

FOR SERVING

1 handful fresh rocket

60 g sun-dried tomatoes, drained
  and chopped

30 ml picked-over chervil

1 handful Parmesan shavings

Make the sauce first. Bring the double cream and mustard to the boil in a small saucepan over medium heat. Season with salt and pepper to taste and reserve until required.

To make the risotto, heat the oil in a pan and sweat the onion until it has softened but not coloured. Add the rice and stir until it is well coated in oil.

Add the white wine to the pan and bring to the boil. Add the stock, ladleful by ladleful, stirring continuously until each batch is absorbed. Continue to add the stock and stir as often as possible until the rice is tender but still retains a bite – this should take around 15 minutes.

To prepare the haddock, poach it in the double cream until the fish has turned opaque. Once cooked, flake the fish and stir it into the risotto along with the poaching cream and the grated Parmesan. Keep warm.

To poach the eggs, bring a deep pan of water to the boil and add the dash of vinegar. Reduce to a gentle simmer. Break the eggs into the water and poach for 3 minutes. Using a slotted spoon, lift each egg out the water and drain on kitchen paper.

To serve, heat the sauce and divide the risotto between four plates. Top each mound of risotto with a poached egg and a spoonful of sauce. Garnish with the rocket leaves, sun-dried tomatoes, chervil and Parmesan shavings before serving.

Serves 4

A well-chilled Blanc de Noir

Kerrievis

Pickled Fish

Few Cape homes would be without their own recipe for *kerrievis*, as pickling was a popular way of preserving fish in the days before refrigerators. Pickled fish is often served with a little salad as a first course, but when served as a main course it is accompanied by a salad of potato and some dressed lettuce leaves. Good Friday seems to be the most popular day on which this dish is served.

2 kg filleted fish, all bones removed and cut into squares of about 6 cm

Seasoned flour

125 ml vegetable oil

PICKLE

4 large onions, halved and then thickly sliced

70 ml vegetable oil

45 ml aromatic mild curry powder

5 ml turmeric

5 ml paprika

5 ml ground coriander

15 ml whole allspice

125 g light brown sugar

15 ml peeled and finely chopped fresh ginger or galangal

15 ml finely chopped seeded chilli

3 bay leaves, cut in strips with scissors

10 ml sea salt

500 ml white wine vinegar

250 ml water

3 fresh bay or lemon leaves

Cook the fish two days ahead of requiring the dish. Pat the fish dry and dip into the seasoned flour. Fry in batches in the hot oil for about 4 minutes on each side or until golden brown and cooked through. As the fillets are cooked, remove and drain on kitchen paper and allow to cool. If desired, the fish can be brushed with oil and baked in an oven preheated to 180 °C for about 25 minutes.

To prepare the pickle, fry the onions gently in the vegetable oil until they are transparent but have not lost their crunch. Add the curry powder, turmeric, paprika and coriander. Fry over gentle heat for a short while to release the aromatic oils from the spices.

Add the remaining ingredients, except the vinegar, water and fresh bay or lemon leaves, and cook gently for 2 minutes. Pour over the vinegar and water gently to prevent splashing. Bring to the boil over high heat, then turn down the heat and simmer the pickle for 10 minutes.

Assemble the dish by pouring a little of the pickle into a glass or ceramic dish. Place a single layer of the fish on top and cover that with pickle. Build up layers of fish and pickle, ending with a layer of pickle. Place the fresh bay or lemon leaves on top. Cover loosely and allow to cool completely. When cold, cover with plastic wrap and refrigerate for two days.

Serve the pickled fish with the marinated onions and a little bit of the sauce.

Serves 6 as a main course or 10 as a starter

 Red Muscadel – please chill it

Nadia Graves' Halibut with Mussels and Chorizo

Nadia Graves has been a friend for some time and has often appeared on my website with her wonderful recipes. She lives with her husband in the South of France, where she has access to a wonderful supply of produce.

500 g mussels

60 ml dry white wine

60 ml water

30 ml extra virgin olive oil, plus a bit extra

2 large potatoes, peeled and sliced about 5 mm thick

1 piece (about 170 g) chorizo, cut into about 16 slices

1 medium onion, diced

2 cloves garlic, crushed

Sea salt and freshly milled black pepper

4 halibut fillets (170 g each) – or substitute with hake

15 ml chopped fresh parsley

Preheat the oven to 200 °C.

Clean the mussels and discard any that may already be open.

Place the wine and water in a large saucepan, bring to the boil and then add the mussels. Cover and boil for 3–4 minutes, until the mussels open.

Drain and reserve the liquid, then strain it to remove any sand and grit.

Discard any mussels that did not open.

Remove and discard the top shell of each mussel. Pour the reserved and strained liquid over the mussels and set aside.

Heat the oil in a large skillet over medium heat. Add the sliced potatoes and chorizo and cook for about 10 minutes until lightly golden and tender.

Add the onion and garlic, then stir in the reserved mussels and liquid. Bring to the boil, then reduce the heat and simmer for 3 minutes. Add salt and freshly milled black pepper to taste.

Meanwhile, rub the fish fillets with a little olive oil. Arrange on a baking tray and place in the oven. Bake for about 10 minutes, depending on the thickness of the fish.

Divide the potatoes, chorizo and mussels between four plates. Arrange a fish fillet on top and sprinkle with parsley.

Enjoy!

Serves 4

 A good Cinsault – chilled

Nicky Fitzgerald's Goan Fish Curry

We have known Nicky Fitzgerald for what seems like forever. She is godmother to our son, Peter, and a Living National Treasure in the hospitality industry. Nicky is also a consummate cook, busy bee and organiser. She and her late husband, Steve, created and operated lodges all over Africa and in India. Her current focus is the fabulous Angama Mara Lodge in Kenya, where she spends a lot of her time. This dish is one of the favourites of the many visitors who stay at the lodge.

4 fish fillets (Angama Mara chefs use Nile perch, but any firm-fleshed white fish works well)

CURRY SAUCE

Vegetable oil for frying

1 large onion, finely chopped

2 cloves garlic, finely chopped

5 ml grated fresh ginger

2 small fresh chillies, seeded and finely chopped

15 ml curry powder

15 ml ground coriander

15 ml paprika

15 ml garam masala (see p. 171)

5 ml turmeric

1 tin (410 g) peeled and chopped tomatoes

30 ml tomato paste

30 ml mango chutney

250 ml coconut milk

Sea salt

FOR SERVING

Fresh coriander, roughly chopped

Chapattis

Steamed rice

Raita (plain yoghurt mixed with grated cucumber)

Mango chutney

Make the curry sauce first. Heat a little vegetable oil and gently fry the onion, garlic, ginger and chillies for at least 10 minutes until soft, taking care not to burn the ingredients.

Add all the dry spices and cook for a further 2 minutes. Add the tomatoes and tomato paste and cook for a further 5 minutes. Finally, add the mango chutney and coconut milk and simmer for 15–20 minutes. Check seasoning and add salt as required.

Preheat the oven to 180 °C.

Heat a frying pan, add a little vegetable oil and brown the fish fillets on both sides. Arrange the fillets in an ovenproof dish and cover with the curry sauce. Bake for 5–7 minutes.

Serve with freshly chopped coriander, chapattis, steamed rice, raita and more mango chutney.

Serves 4

 Bukettraube would be a great choice

Poultry

Growing up on a farm, we had chicken for lunch almost
every Sunday. They weren't the dainty little things you
find on the supermarket shelves today, but at times large
cockerels whose crowing at dawn was more than we could
bear. My long recipe for the family Chicken Pie, my restyled
Louis Leipoldt Chicken Curry and the Duck Rice, served by
Patricia Coutinho in Lisbon, are among my favourite
dishes in this book.

Chicken Liver Toasts, Tuscan Style

I made these once at the African Relish cookery school in the Karoo town of Prince Albert for a course that I led there. It was at a time when I was very influenced by Anna Del Conte's food. Still am. The students loved it. It's a bit of a heritage dish for me as my mother cooked lamb's liver with onions and vinegar for lunch every Saturday.

400 g chicken livers, cleaned

60 ml sunflower, rice bran or canola oil

½ stick celery, very finely chopped

1 small onion, very finely chopped

2 fat cloves garlic, very finely chopped

45 ml finely chopped fresh parsley,
    plus extra for garnishing

15 ml tomato paste

90 ml dry white wine

Sea salt and freshly milled
    black pepper

4 anchovy fillets, chopped

30 ml butter

15 ml capers, rinsed well and chopped

Extra virgin olive oil for the bread

4 slices (not too thick) artisanal bread

Preheat the oven to 200 °C.

Make sure the livers are well cleaned and then cut them into small squares.

Heat the oil in a sauté pan over low heat and add the celery, onion, garlic and parsley. Sauté for about 8 minutes until soft.

Add the chicken livers and cook them gently until nearly done. Stir in the tomato paste and cook for a minute or so. Pour in the wine, and season with the sea salt and plenty of freshly milled black pepper. Turn up the heat, add the anchovy fillets and simmer gently for 5–8 minutes. Finally, add the butter and capers and swirl the pan to mix well.

In the meantime, brush some olive oil onto the slices of bread. Place on a baking tray and bake them in the oven until crunchy.

Dish the livers onto the toasted bread and garnish with some extra chopped parsley.

Serves 4

 Nothing quite like a glass of chilled Lambrusco here

Brick Chicken, a Tuscan Tradition

Brick chicken is named after the bricks that are placed on top of the chicken while it is cooking in the pan! I saw steak houses put weights on steak, so I thought I would try it on chicken. Although very excited at the time thinking that I had 'invented' something, I later found out it was a Tuscan method of cooking known as Sotto Mattone.

1 chicken (1.5–2 kg)

6 sprigs fresh thyme, leaves picked

Sea salt and freshly milled black pepper

30 ml extra virgin olive oil

85–100 ml NOMU Chicken Stock (prepared as per packaging instructions)

15 ml lemon juice

Grated rind of ½ lemon

100 ml fresh cream

45 ml chopped fresh flat-leaf parsley or sprigs fresh thyme for garnishing

Cut the chicken in half and remove the backbone, ribcage and thigh bones. (These can be used to enrich the stock – just simmer the bones and stock together for about 20 minutes.) Season the chicken well on both sides with thyme, sea salt and freshly milled black pepper. Marinate for 4 hours or overnight in the refrigerator. Return to room temperature before cooking the chicken.

Heat the oil in a large saucepan. When the oil is very hot, place the two chicken halves in the pan, skin-side down. Place a brick* on each half to weigh the chicken down. Immediately reduce the heat to medium-high and cook the chicken for 18–20 minutes until the skin is golden brown and crisp.

Remove the bricks, turn over the chicken halves with a pair of tongs and pour off the excess oil. Pour the stock, lemon juice and lemon rind around the chicken and cook for 5–8 minutes. Swirl in the cream and shake the pan to form an emulsion. Garnish with the parsley or sprigs of thyme and serve the chicken with the pan juices.

 Serves 4

 I would go with a Sauvignon Blanc here to cut the creaminess

* You will need two standard builders' bricks covered in a thick layer of aluminium foil.

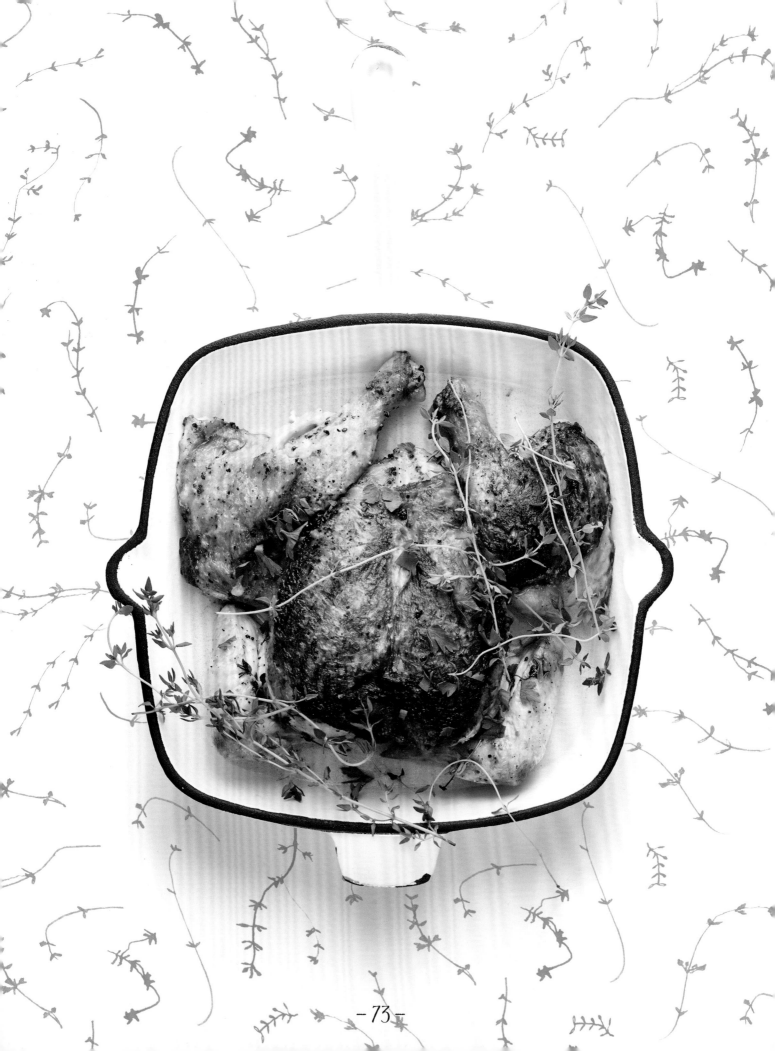

Chicken and Corn Nachos

This nachos recipe by Christine Capendale is one she sent me to use on my website. The dish is so utterly delicious and a huge treat that I could not leave it out. It takes about 15 minutes to prepare and even though it uses several convenience products, it is still quite a healthy meal. This is the perfect stay-at-home Friday dinner.

30 ml extra virgin olive oil

4 chicken breast fillets, cut into strips

Sea salt and freshly milled
  black pepper

1 red onion, sliced

2 cloves garlic, crushed

150 g cherry tomatoes, halved

80 g sun-dried tomatoes, drained
  and chopped

½ tin (200 g) whole kernel corn,
  drained

350 g plain nachos

160 ml mild tomato salsa or
  Peppadew salsa

250 ml grated Cheddar cheese
  (or use half Cheddar and half
  mozzarella)

2 avocados, peeled and sliced

15 ml lime juice

120 ml sour cream

60 ml thinly sliced jalapeño chillies
  (optional)

Preheat the oven to 180 °C.

Heat the oil in a frying pan over medium heat and cook the chicken strips until done and golden brown. Season with salt and freshly milled black pepper and remove from the pan.

Add the onion and garlic to the same pan and cook until soft and starting to caramelise. Season with salt and pepper and remove from the heat.

Add the chicken to the onion mixture along with the cherry tomatoes, sun-dried tomatoes and corn.

Divide the nachos between four ovenproof serving bowls (or one large dish) and spoon the chicken mixture over the nachos. Spoon over the salsa and top with the grated cheese.

Bake in the oven for about 12 minutes until the cheese has melted and is golden brown.

Season the avocados with salt and pepper and drizzle over the lime juice.

Serve the nachos immediately with the sour cream, avocados and jalapeño chillies (if using) on the side or piled on top.

Serves 4

 Have to have a Mexican beer here, Corona is perfect

Outydse Hoenderpastei

Old-fashioned Chicken Pie

While this is not strictly a Malay dish at the Cape – some versions have diced ham in them, which would point to Europe – chicken pies thickened with sago were used at celebratory occasions such as weddings. My mother used a recipe from an old friend of hers – Mrs Norton – who as an Afrikaans-speaking person impressed us hugely as children by doing the crossword puzzle in the London *Times*.
This was an especially exotic recipe as you used lard ('it makes the pastry shorter') and chilled bottled soda water ('the bubbles make the pastry lighter', said Mrs Norton). We'd often use this same pastry to make a Cape gooseberry pie for Sunday lunch.

PASTRY

500 g cake flour
A generous pinch of sea salt
250 g well-chilled butter, cubed
130 g well-chilled lard, cubed
Up to 180 ml chilled soda water

CHICKEN FILLING

(My version of a Phillippa Cheifitz recipe)
2 free-range chickens
Sea salt and freshly milled black pepper
500 ml full-bodied off-dry white
    wine (Chenin Blanc)
250 ml good-quality
    chicken stock
2 onions, finely sliced
2 sticks celery, finely sliced
2 large carrots, peeled and
    finely sliced
Some chopped celery
    leaves
Some whole parsley
    stalks
2 bay leaves
A little melted butter

SAUCE

1 whole peeled onion
6 whole cloves
3 blades mace
650 ml full-cream milk
125 g butter
60 g cake flour
100 ml fresh cream
200 g cooked ham, diced
60 ml chopped fresh parsley
15 ml Dijon mustard

PASTRY GLAZE

1 free-range egg white
A pinch of sea salt

FOR THE PASTRY

Sift the flour and salt twice into the bowl of a food processor. Toss in the butter and lard and pulse using a plastic blade until the mixture resembles fine breadcrumbs.

Pour in two-thirds of the soda water and pulse until the mixture forms a ball. Add more water a little at a time if necessary, until all the flour is taken up. Dust with extra flour, cover with plastic wrap and chill in the refrigerator for about 30 minutes.

Place the dough on a lightly floured pastry board and, with the flat of your hand, press it out into a rectangular shape about 2 cm thick.

Keeping the board dusted with flour and using a floured rolling pin, roll out the dough into a strip about 35 cm long and about 15 cm wide. Fold in three and turn the open end towards you. Repeat the rolling process four times and, when finished, fold it in three again. Rest in the refrigerator for up to two days or seal well and freeze.

FOR THE CHICKEN FILLING

Preheat the oven to 180 °C.

Truss the chickens after seasoning them well inside with salt and freshly milled black pepper.

Pour the wine and chicken stock into a roasting dish. Add the vegetables and the aromatics, making a bed for the chickens. Place the chickens on top, brush with the melted butter and season with salt and freshly milled black pepper. Cover with foil and roast for 75–90 minutes or until all redness around the leg joints has disappeared.

FOR THE SAUCE

Take the whole peeled onion and stick the cloves into it. Place in a saucepan with the blades of mace and pour over the milk. Heat the milk until just below boiling, then cover and remove from the heat and allow to infuse until you need it.

Remove the skin and the bones from the chickens and place the meat back into the roasting dish. Simmer until the stock has reduced to 250 ml. Strain and set aside for later use in the sauce. Cut the meat into chunks and place it into a 2-litre pie dish.

Continue preparing the sauce. Strain the onion and mace from the milk. Melt the butter over medium heat, whisk in the flour and cook for a short while. Increase the heat and whisk in the reserved strained stock, the infused milk and the cream. Bring to the boil and simmer for a while to cook the flour. Stir in the ham, parsley and mustard. Taste for seasoning and add more salt and pepper if necessary. Pour the sauce over the chicken and mix well. Cover and allow to cool.

When you are ready to bake the pie, preheat the oven to 220 °C.

Roll out the pastry so that it is slightly larger than the pie dish. Cover the pie filling with the pastry, lining the edge of the dish with a strip of pastry to give the pie a thick edge. Decorate with pastry leaves from the offcuts and scallop the edges. Use a pie bird or cut some vent holes to allow steam to escape.

FOR THE PASTRY GLAZE

Whisk the egg white with the salt and brush it over the pastry. Bake for 20 minutes. Reduce the heat to 190 °C and bake for a further 20 minutes or until the pie is nicely golden brown on top.

Serves 8

Chenin Blanc, no doubt about it

Hoenderbiryani

Chicken Biryani

Biriani (also spelled breyani and biryani in the Cape) is Indian of origin, but has been embraced in the Cape by the Muslim community as a dish of their own. This is a generous festive dish. Traditionally, it was perfumed with saffron, but today it is more likely to be coloured using turmeric, a far more economical option.

400 g long-grain rice

2 litres cold water

15 ml sea salt

2.5 ml turmeric

30 ml warm milk

4 medium onions, 1 finely chopped and 3 sliced into rings

4 cloves garlic, finely chopped

4 cm piece fresh ginger, peeled

60 ml sunflower oil

90 ml seedless raisins or sultanas

90 ml slivered almonds

1.5 kg skinned and boned chicken thighs, halved

250 ml plain yoghurt

Sea salt and freshly milled black pepper

Chopped fresh parsley or coriander leaves

3 free-range eggs, hard-boiled, peeled and quartered

SPICE MIX

6 whole cloves

5 ml cardamom seeds

10 ml cumin seeds

10 ml coriander seeds

4 cm cinnamon quill

A good grating of nutmeg

2.5 ml cayenne pepper

Wash the rice well, changing the water frequently. Place in a large bowl and pour over the 2 litres cold water and add the salt. Allow to stand for about 2 hours. This will keep the rice as white as possible and keep the grains separate.

Dissolve the turmeric in the warm milk and set aside.

Put the one chopped onion, the garlic and the ginger with a little water into the bowl of a blender and process until you have a smooth paste. Set aside.

Heat the oil in a heavy-bottomed casserole and fry the slices of onion until they are brown and crisp. Drain on kitchen paper and set aside.

In the same pan using the same oil, repeat the process with the raisins or sultanas and the almonds, frying them for a short while until the raisins or sultanas fatten up and the almonds are a light golden brown. Drain on kitchen paper and set aside.

Preheat the oven to 180 °C.

Brown the chicken pieces all over in the same oil. Drain and set aside on kitchen paper.

Add more oil to the casserole only if necessary and add the onion-garlic-ginger paste and fry gently, adding a little water if necessary to prevent sticking, until the paste takes on a light brown colour. Add the yoghurt a spoonful at a time, stirring well between each addition. Place the chicken pieces on top of the yoghurt. Cover the casserole and bake in the oven for 30 minutes.

In the meantime, put the spice mix ingredients into a pestle and mortar and pound together or grind in a spice or coffee grinder until quite fine. When the chicken has simmered for 30 minutes, remove any oil from the top using a spoon or kitchen paper. Sprinkle over the spice mixture and season with salt and freshly milled black pepper to taste, turn the chicken pieces over and bake, covered, for a further 30 minutes.

Meanwhile, rinse the rice again and boil in lots of well salted water for 6 minutes.

Pile the rice on top of the chicken in the casserole, in a pyramid, and then dribble the turmeric milk down the sides. Sprinkle over a few of the browned onions. Cover closely with foil and the lid and bake in the oven for a further 20 minutes.

When ready to serve, mix the chicken and the rice together gently with the chopped parsley or coriander and garnish with the remaining browned onions, the raisins or sultanas and almonds. Place the egg quarters decoratively on top. Serve with a green vegetable, such as shredded steamed cabbage flavoured with nutmeg.

Serves 6

Ooh – a lovely chilled Pale Ale

Old Cape Chicken Curry, in the Style of Louis Leipoldt

I wanted to make a 'new' chicken curry, so I had a look at one of Louis Leipoldt's cookery books and found a chicken curry recipe. It must be remembered that when Louis Leipoldt was a student of medicine in London, he also worked in the basement kitchens at the Savoy Hotel, under Auguste Escoffier, so he knew what he was doing behind the stove. However good a poet and writer he may have been, he was just the opposite whenever he wrote a recipe. He used no quantities, no temperatures, no dish sizes. He once suggested baking pastry in an oven 'hot enough to roast a guinea fowl'. So, I took his sketchy description and turned it into a recipe that the modern cook could use to get the sort of flavour of which I hoped Leipoldt would approve.

In his compilation, *Leipoldt's Food and Wine*, Trevor Emslie says: 'As is evident from the text, Leipoldt was not a stickler for precision measurement in the kitchen.' How true.

60 g butter

6 chicken thighs, skin on and thoroughly dry

2 large onions, cut into wedges (see Cook's Note)

2 cloves garlic, finely chopped

1 walnut-size piece fresh ginger, peeled and finely chopped

15 ml medium curry powder or garam masala (see p. 171)

Juice of 1 lemon

1 Granny Smith apple, cored and thinly sliced

15 ml coconut sugar (or use ordinary brown sugar)

250 ml coconut milk

Water or chicken stock

Sea salt and freshly milled black pepper

Have ready a comfortable-size enamelled cast-iron casserole with a lid.

In it, heat the butter and brown the chicken thighs, skin-side first. Do this over relatively low heat. Remove the chicken from the casserole and set aside.

Add the onion wedges to the casserole and cook them very slowly over medium heat to get them golden brown This takes time – 15–20 minutes. Halfway through, add the garlic and ginger. When ready, add the curry powder and cook slowly again to allow the spice to become aromatic. Add the lemon juice (Leipoldt used tamarind water), apple, sugar and coconut milk.

Return the chicken to the casserole and almost cover with just-boiled water or chicken stock. Season well, cover, bring to the boil and then cook on a heat diffuser for about 2 hours, giving it a good shake each time you walk past the stove. When ready, taste and reseason.

Serve with steamed white rice and chutney.

Serves 2 hungry people or 3 as part of a bigger meal

 Try a chilled Late Harvest White here, the curry could do with a little sweetness

COOK'S NOTE

I usually cut the root and top end off for wedging, cut in half top to bottom and then cut each half into about eight wedges. This gives a bit of texture to the dish.

Dianne Bibby's Cape Malay Chicken Meatball Curry

Here is one of our finest food creators, food writers, food photographers and cookbook authors. Dianne and I have been friends for a long time, and I love using her fine food on my website with my wine recommendations. That she is a truly lovely woman is a huge bonus.

Dianne says: 'Inspired by the flavours of a traditional Cape Malay curry, here is my playful take on one of South Africa's most loved curries. Leaning on creative latitude, I've added grated baby marrows to the meatball mixture. It lightens the texture somewhat and pairs well with the chicken. When thinking about what to serve alongside, chutney was the obvious choice. Just then, my eye fell to the apples on the counter, which is how this throw-together apple chutney came to be. The flavour is delightfully clean and fresh with a zingy-ness that does wonders to counter the rich tomato sauce. We all agreed it was the making of the dish.'

MEATBALLS

500 g chicken mince

3 medium baby marrows, grated and excess water pressed out

250 ml fresh breadcrumbs

5 ml ground coriander

5 ml ground cumin

4 ml fine sea salt

SAUCE

Coconut oil for frying

1 large onion, finely diced

2 cloves garlic, minced

15 ml grated fresh ginger

2.5 ml dried chilli flakes

12.5 ml garam masala (see p. 171)

5 ml turmeric

2 pieces stick cinnamon

5 ml brown sugar

30 ml tomato paste

1 tin (410 g) chopped tomatoes

125 ml chicken stock

250 ml coconut milk

Sea salt and freshly milled black pepper

To make the meatballs, combine all the ingredients in a mixing bowl. Roll into even-size balls. The mixture makes 22–24.

Heat 15 ml coconut oil in a wide-based pan. Brown the meatballs on all sides, then remove from the pan and set aside.

To make the sauce, add a little more coconut oil to the pan and sauté the onion for 6–8 minutes until softened. Stir in the garlic and ginger and cook for another minute or two. Add the spices, mix through and toast for just a minute to intensify the flavours. At this point the onions will look dry and crumbly.

Add all the remaining sauce ingredients, stir through and bring the sauce to the boil. Return the meatballs to the pan, cover and simmer for around 25 minutes until the sauce has thickened and reduced.

To make the salsa, combine the apple, cucumber, spring onions and herbs in a small bowl. Drizzle with the olive oil and lemon juice, then season lightly with salt and pepper. Toss to combine.

Serve the curry with steamed rice or noodles, and the salsa on the side.

 Serves 4

 A good fruity IPA

CRUNCHY APPLE SALSA

1 Pink Lady apple, skin on, diced

½ cucumber, seeded and cut into fine dice

3 spring onions, sliced

1 handful fresh flat-leaf parsley and mint,
    roughly chopped

40 ml extra virgin olive oil

30 ml lemon juice

Sea salt flakes and freshly milled black pepper

1 handful micro herbs for garnishing (optional)

Arroz de Pato

Portuguese Duck Rice

On my first visit to Portugal in 2008, I fell totally in love with the country, its people, its food and its wine. I went back in 2010 to co-author a book on Portuguese wine with Anibal Coutinho, a well-known expert on the Portuguese wine industry. At dinner in his home one evening, his wife, Patricia, served us the finest examples of Portuguese family food. I had not realised until then that Portugal grows fine rice. This dish at times uses octopus, chicken or beef.

1 duck, halved

Sea salt and freshly milled black pepper

250 ml red wine

250 ml water

1 sprig fresh rosemary

1 bay leaf

3 whole cloves

1 onion, thinly sliced

150 g rashers bacon or pancetta, chopped

1 chorizo, half finely chopped, half sliced

30 ml olive oil (if needed)

1 onion, chopped

2 cloves garlic, chopped

500 g long-grain rice

NOMU Chicken Stock (enough to cover the rice and prepared according to packaging instructions)

8 soft dried apricots, finely chopped

150 g high-fat easy-melting cheese, such as Gruyère, Emmentaler or Jarlsberg, grated

1 small bunch fresh thyme, leaves picked

Season the duck well on both sides. Place it in an enamelled cast-iron casserole with the red wine, water, rosemary, bay leaf and cloves. Bring to the boil and then turn the heat to low and allow to cook until the meat comes off the bone. This could take an hour.

Remove the duck from the casserole and allow to cool slightly. Take the meat and skin off the bones, shred and set aside. Reserve any liquid in the casserole for later, but remember to remove the cloves. Wipe the casserole with kitchen paper.

In the same casserole, gently fry the sliced onion, the bacon or pancetta and the chopped chorizo until it browns – there should be enough fat not to need more, but add a little splash of olive oil if you feel you do. Add the chopped onion and cook gently until it is soft and golden, and then add the garlic. Add the shredded duck meat and skin. Allow to cook together for about 5 minutes over low heat.

Preheat the oven to 170 °C.

Add the rice to the casserole and mix well. Add the reserved pan juices and enough extra chicken stock to just cover the rice. Stir in the apricots. Place the lid on the casserole and bake in the oven for about 20 minutes. Check after 15 minutes and add more stock or red wine to prevent it from being too dry. When done, place the sliced chorizo on top and sprinkle with the cheese. Return to the oven for 15 minutes with the lid off until the top is golden and all the stock has been absorbed.

Garnish with the thyme leaves just before serving with a crisp well-dressed salad and some crunchy bread. We had folar de pascoa, a traditional Portuguese Easter bread.

Serves 4

If you can land one, a red from the Douro Valley in Northern Portugal

Pot-roasted Turkey Breast with a Berry Sauce

Turkey is a neglected protein in South Africa, yet so good. Turkey mince can be turned into all sorts of things. The breed of turkey we have in South Africa is the brown turkey. The feathers leave little brown marks on the skin, which some people don't like. I am pleased that turkey meat is making an appearance again in the marketplace. One Christmas some time ago, I pot-roasted a turkey breast. I'd still love to try to roast some legs like lamb shanks.

1 turkey breast weighing about 1.5 kg

Sea salt and freshly milled
    black pepper

Grated rind of 1 lemon

200 g thinly sliced streaky bacon

Extra virgin olive oil

80 g butter

1 large onion, sliced

1 large carrot, peeled and sliced

1 stick celery, sliced

Some sprigs fresh parsley

30 ml cranberry jelly or
    blackcurrant jam

30 ml blackcurrant vinegar or
    red wine vinegar

50 ml crème de cassis

500 ml ready-made gravy (Ina
    Paarman's is perfect)

Sprigs fresh rosemary for garnishing

Using a sharp knife, make a series of thin cuts across the turkey breast to prevent shrinkage during roasting. Season the meat well with sea salt, black pepper and the lemon rind. Fold over the flap to form a 'joint' of meat of even thickness. Lay the bacon slices over the top and then tie the joint with four pieces of string across the width and two across the length.

Pour in enough olive oil to cover the base of a heavy-bottomed casserole and heat until almost smoking. Swirl in the butter and then immediately brown the turkey on all sides. Set aside.

Add the onion to the casserole and cook gently for a while until it turns light brown. Add the carrot and celery and braise for a while. Make a little heap of the vegetables in the middle of the casserole and put the parsley and the turkey on top. Place the lid on top and pot-roast the turkey for 80 minutes over very low heat. Remove the turkey from the casserole and set aside to rest for about 10 minutes.

Now you need to get inventive with the sauce. Pour everything out of the casserole and set it aside. Swirl the cranberry jelly or blackcurrant jam and the vinegar together in the casserole. Reduce this over medium heat and allow it to caramelise. Deglaze with the crème de cassis. Add the gravy and the reserved pan juices and vegetables. Using a potato masher, break down the vegetables so that there is still a bit of texture in the sauce.

Slice the turkey, garnish with sprigs of rosemary and serve with the sauce.

Serves 4

 Merlot will love the fruit in the berry sauce

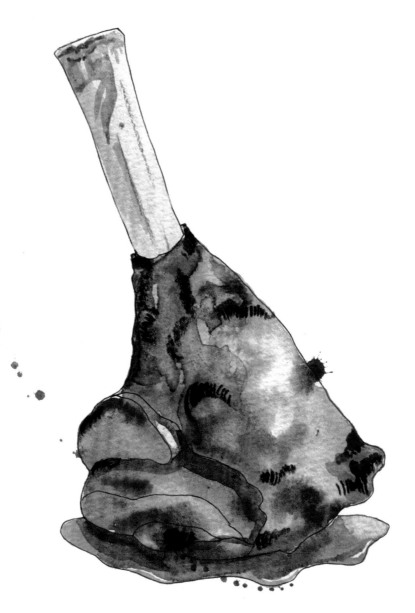

Beef, Lamb, Pork and Offal

How important is meat in the average South African home? As a boy, every Sunday a dish of meat would be taken out of the old Aga stove in the kitchen, steaming savoury with all its little burned and caramelly edges and deep, dark, soft onions, which formed part of the unctuous real old-fashioned gravy. There are some really delicious dishes in this chapter, along with a couple of my reconstructions of traditional dishes. Here you'll find a great Bobotie, Lamb with Quinces, and the Lamb and Cabbage Bredie, which the photography crew set upon and devoured immediately after the shoot.

Bobotie

Curried Beef Mince Timbale

This is probably the most widely known and loved of all South African dishes. It has its origins at the Cape in the 17th century when Malay slaves, who were brought to the Cape by Dutch Settlers, introduced their unique style of cooking, infused with the spices of the East. In earlier times, it was made as a Monday supper dish from leftover roast lamb or beef (usually the remains of a Sunday roast), but in the South African home of today, raw beef mince is usually used. Bobotie is traditionally served in an earthenware casserole with yellow raisin rice, toasted coconut, sliced banana, a finely chopped tomato and onion sambal, and a fruity chutney.

1 thick slice white bread, crusts removed

250 ml cold milk

30 ml sunflower or peanut oil

15 ml butter

2 medium onions, finely chopped

2 fat cloves garlic, chopped

15 ml medium aromatic curry powder

5 ml turmeric

30 ml white wine vinegar, tamarind juice or lemon juice

1 kg beef mince (a portion of this could be minced fatty mutton)

45 ml fruity chutney

125 ml ground almonds

75 g unbleached seedless sultanas

Grated rind of 1 lemon and 1 orange (no white pith)

15 ml light brown sugar or palm sugar

4 bay leaves

Sea salt and freshly milled black pepper

2 jumbo free-range eggs

A knife point of turmeric (optional)

6 fresh lemon leaves for garnishing

Soak the slice of bread in the milk and, when saturated, squeeze dry in a sieve. Set aside. Reserve the milk to make the custard topping.

Preheat the oven to 180 °C.

In a heavy-bottomed saucepan, heat the oil and the butter and start browning the onions over medium heat. After a while, add the garlic and continue cooking slowly until the mixture is a light golden brown.

Add the curry powder, turmeric and white wine vinegar, tamarind juice or lemon juice and cook for a few minutes to release the aromatic oils of the spices. Add the beef mince and stir with a spoon to break it up. Keep stirring until it loses its red colour. Add the chutney, almonds, sultanas, grated rinds, sugar, bay leaves and seasoning. Add one of the eggs, beaten, and the soaked bread and mix well. Taste and reseason if necessary.

Spoon the mince mixture into a shallow ovenproof dish and smooth off the top. Cover and bake for 1½ hours. Turn down the oven temperature to 150 °C to cook the topping.

To make the topping, whisk the remaining egg into the reserved milk, season and strain if required. At this point you could add a knife point of turmeric to the milk just to give the topping a yellow colour. When the bobotie comes out of the oven, pour over the topping. Garnish in a pattern with the lemon leaves and return to the oven for a further 30 minutes or until the topping has set.

Serve with the suggested accompaniments.

Serves 6

 Here you want a young and frisky Pinotage

Ming-Cheau Lin's Teppan Beef

Ming-Cheau Lin is of Taiwanese origin and spent time in Bloemfontein. She is a great cook, as her book _Just Add Rice_ attests. She cooked with me once on Breakfast TV. Sadly, she is now living in California, lost to us.

PICKLED CABBAGE AND CARROTS

300 g cabbage, chopped or shredded into rough, chunky 3 cm pieces

125 ml sea salt

2 carrots, peeled and sliced 2.5 mm thick

2 red or green chillies, halved lengthwise (leave the seeds in)

500 ml rice vinegar or spirit vinegar

125 ml water

125 ml sugar

TEPPAN BEEF

45 ml soy sauce

15 ml light brown sugar

30 ml water

30 ml cornflour

400 g beef strips

30 ml butter

2 onions, sliced into chunks

60 ml cooking oil

5 ml freshly milled black pepper

FOR SERVING

Rice

Fried free-range eggs

Chopped fresh coriander and spring onions for garnishing (optional)

Make the pickle first. Place the cabbage in a plastic bag, add the salt and give it a good shake. Let it sit for 1 hour, then rinse the salt off the cabbage.

Arrange the cabbage, carrots and chillies in sterilised glass jars.

Heat the vinegar and water in a saucepan on the stove. Add the sugar, let it melt and bring to a simmer, then remove from the heat. Pour the hot pickling liquid into the jars, seal them and set aside in a dark place.

If you want to eat the pickle quite soon, give it 1 hour of pickling. But if you want the flavours to develop fully, give it a day's rest. Refrigerate the pickles once opened.

To make the teppan beef, mix the soy sauce, sugar, water and cornflour together to make a marinade.

Add the beef strips and work the marinade into the meat. Set aside in the refrigerator for at least 30 minutes.

Melt the butter in a wok (or frying pan) over low heat and cook the onions until slightly translucent.

Add the oil to the marinated beef and mix it in. Turn the heat up in the wok and stir-fry the meat until done, adding the pepper and more soy sauce to taste.

Serve with rice and a fried egg, garnished with coriander and spring onions, and the pickled cabbage, carrots and chillies on the side.

 Serves 4

 You want a plush berried Shiraz here

COOK'S NOTES

This dish works just as well using chicken, lamb, seafood or silken tofu instead of the beef. You can also add green or red peppers and serve with stir-fried egg noodles instead of rice.

Christine Capendale's Beef Fillet with Burrata and a Caper Sauce

Christine Capendale is a truly busy cook and food writer. Her latest book, *Meals*, was published in 2019. An internet friend, I often use her recipes as recommendations to partner my wine reviews.

Christine says, 'This dish looks sumptuous served on a large platter for everybody to help themselves. Serve it accompanied with crispy potato wedges. If you cannot find burrata, use any other fresh, soft mozzarella cheese, such as fior di latte, bocconcini or nodini.'

40 ml extra virgin olive oil

Sea salt and freshly milled black pepper

1 kg beef fillet

1 large onion, sliced

30 ml capers, drained and rinsed, lightly chopped

50 ml lemon juice

5 ml honey

300 g mixed exotic baby tomatoes (yellow, red and green varieties)

15 ml chopped chives

250 g burrata

80 ml crispy onions (store-bought or see p. 78)

Fresh basil and rocket for garnishing

Preheat the oven to 200 °C.

Mix 15 ml of the olive oil with sea salt and milled black pepper and rub into the beef fillet.

Heat a griddle pan over medium heat and grill the fillet, turning, for about 6 minutes until browned on all sides. Transfer the fillet to a roasting pan and roast for 10–15 minutes in the preheated oven until cooked to your liking. Rest the meat for 10 minutes before cutting it into thick slices. Drizzle with the pan juices.

While the fillet is roasting, heat another 20 ml olive oil in a frying pan over medium heat and add the onion and capers. Cook until the onion is soft and the capers become crispy. Add the lemon juice and honey and reduce the sauce. Season with sea salt and milled black pepper.

Halve and quarter the baby tomatoes and mix them with the remaining 5 ml olive oil and the chives. Season with sea salt and milled black pepper.

To serve, place the meat on a large serving platter and drizzle with the caper sauce. Add the tomatoes to the platter and top with the burrata and crispy onions. Garnish with fresh basil and rocket.

 Serves 4

 Ah! A brilliant Stellenbosch Cabernet Sauvignon

An Indian Lamb Curry, My Way

This is a curry that requires a cool cucumber and mint raita, bhuni hui pyaz (crisp browned onions), toasty warm naan breads and steaming basmati rice perfumed with garam masala. You will find a recipe for garam masala on page 171. Don't be tempted to use a fruity Cape-style curry powder.

2 kg lamb shanks, bone in, sliced, or lamb knuckles

Seasoned flour

A little sunflower oil

60 g butter

2 large onions, finely chopped

6 fat cloves garlic, finely chopped

1 fat thumb-size piece fresh ginger, peeled and finely chopped

45 ml garam masala (which gives a hottish sauce)

1 tin (410 g) whole peeled tomatoes, pressed

1 tin (400 ml) coconut milk

100 ml water

200 ml plain yoghurt

Sea salt

Have ready a plate covered thinly with the well-seasoned flour. Dunk the pieces of lamb in the flour, then shake off the excess and set aside on a plate.

Heat a thin layer of oil in a large ovenproof casserole over medium heat, then brown the lamb pieces in batches until well coloured all over. Do not crowd the casserole, otherwise the lamb will 'stew' rather than brown. Be patient – use fewer pieces and get them nicely brown. Set aside on a plate.

Preheat the oven to 180 °C.

Pour off the excess oil from the casserole and swirl in the butter. Cook the onions over medium heat until light golden brown. Add the garlic and ginger and cook for a short while. Sprinkle over the garam masala and stir-fry for a while to release the flavours from the spices.

Add the tomatoes, coconut milk, water and yoghurt. Bring to a simmer, taste and then add salt if required. Return the lamb pieces to the casserole with any juice that may have collected on the plate. Cover with a paper cartouche and place in the oven – untouched – for 2 hours.

Remove from the oven and test for doneness and seasoning. Adjust if necessary and cook for a bit longer if required. If you have the time, remove it from the oven, cool and refrigerate overnight. Next day, scrape the fat off the top and return the casserole to a 180 °C oven to cook for a further hour or until tender. (If you don't have time to wait until the following day, simply cook for another hour.)

Serve with the accompaniments suggested above.

Serves 4

 Cobra, Kingfisher, Simba or any Indian Beer

Tamatiebredie

Tomato and Lamb Stew

Bredie, both the word and the stew, is of Malay origin. A bredie is a thick, fully flavoured meat stew, usually made from a fattier cut of lamb and named for the vegetable that is the other main ingredient. Green or dried beans, tomatoes, pumpkin and even quinces, cabbage or cauliflower are regular ingredients, with potatoes used to thicken the sauce. Waterblommetjies (*Aponogeton distachyos*), found in ponds and dams in the Cape in early spring, make a delicious bredie, which is usually flavoured with wild sorrel juice (see p. 110).

This is my version of this dish.

45 ml sunflower oil

1.5 kg lamb (⅓ thick rib – bone in, ⅔ deboned shoulder)

3 medium onions, chopped

2 cloves garlic, sliced

2 cm piece fresh ginger, peeled and finely chopped

2 cardamom pods

4 coriander seeds

6 black peppercorns

5 ml fennel seeds

10 ml crushed fresh thyme leaves

5 ml chopped fresh marjoram

2 small red or green chillies, seeded and chopped

Sea salt, freshly milled black pepper and grated nutmeg

500 ml demi-glace or NOMU Beef Stock (prepared according to packaging instructions)

2–3 tins (410 g each) peeled and chopped tomatoes

500 g medium potatoes, peeled and quartered

15 ml mild fruit chutney

15 ml soft brown sugar

Heat the oil in an enamelled cast-iron casserole over medium heat, then brown all the meat in batches. Remove the pieces with a slotted spoon and drain on kitchen paper.

In the same casserole, fry the onions very gently in the oil for a while, then add the garlic and ginger and fry until golden. Add a little more oil, though only if necessary. Just before the onions are done, add the cardamom, coriander, peppercorns, fennel, thyme, marjoram and chillies. Stir-fry for a short while. Pour off any excess oil before continuing.

Return the meat to the casserole and season lightly with salt, freshly milled black pepper and nutmeg. Add the demi-glace or stock and cover. Braise gently over low heat on a heat diffuser for 1½ hours – check to make sure it doesn't catch and burn. Alternatively, cook in a 180 °C oven for 1½ hours.

Remove from the stove or oven. If you have the time, cool quickly and refrigerate overnight – this step matures the flavours. It also gives you the opportunity to remove the cold, solidified fat off the top and helps to tenderise the meat. (If you don't have time to wait until the following day, simply cook for another 1½ hours.)

The next day, reheat the casserole gently in a 180 °C oven before adding the tinned tomatoes and potatoes. Cook for 1½ hours or until the meat is tender. Check occasionally and add a little more stock if too dry.

Stir gently to mix through well. Add the chutney and brown sugar, and reseason with salt and freshly milled black pepper if necessary. Serve with steamed white rice.

Serves 6

 Just screaming for a good, soft, plummy Merlot

Denningvleis

Spiced Fricassée of Lamb

Dendeng is a Malay word for meat cut in slices, cured with salt and spices, dried in the sun and then grilled with coconut oil. **Dendengvleis** made from the meat of a water buffalo was served as a main course in the Batavian **rijsttafel. Denningvleis** is one of the oldest dishes and a firm favourite of the people of the Cape, using interesting combinations of spices. It is usually served with steamed white rice.

The old Cape recipes all call for 'fat leg of mutton meat'. My recipe uses shoulder and a little of the fat would certainly add to the flavour.

3 large onions, very thinly sliced

4 large cloves garlic, chopped

1 chilli, seeded and finely chopped

A little vegetable oil for frying

1 kg deboned shoulder of lamb, cut into 2.5 cm cubes

3 bay leaves

5 whole cloves

5 whole allspice

Sea salt and freshly milled black pepper

30 ml broken-up tamarind

2.5 ml freshly grated nutmeg

Fresh coriander and sliced chilli for garnishing (optional)

In a heavy-bottomed casserole with a tight-fitting lid, gently fry the onions, garlic and chilli in the oil until the onions are soft and transparent.

Wash the meat in fresh water (to provide a little moisture to the steaming process) and then place on top of the onion mixture. Add the bay leaves, cloves, allspice, salt and freshly milled black pepper to taste. Cover with a round of greaseproof paper and the lid of the casserole and steam gently over low heat for about 45 minutes. Check from time to time to ensure that the meat is not cooking dry or burning. Add very little water or lamb stock if necessary.

Meanwhile, soak the broken-up tamarind in about 45 ml boiling water. Strain and set aside for later use.

After the 45 minutes, sprinkle over the tamarind water and the nutmeg. If you are not able to get tamarind, use half lemon juice or vinegar and half water.

Simmer again with the lid on for a further 15 minutes, then remove the whole spices, and reseason if necessary.

Garnish if desired with fresh coriander and sliced chilli, and serve with steamed white rice.

Serves 6

What does one serve with a dish originally made from buffalo? Cinsault, it rhymes!

Meeta K. Wolff's Punjabi-style Curried Lamb and Peas

(Keema Matar)

Meeta Wolff and I are the perfect example of a warm internet friendship. Meeta lives in Weimar in Germany with her husband, Thomas, and their son, Soenen. A highly talented food writer, recipe developer and photographer, Meeta regularly leads food photography workshops in Europe and in Dubai, where her parents live. Her website, which is well worth a visit, is www.whatsforlunchhoney.net

15 ml ghee

Whole garam masala:
    4 whole cloves, 4 cardamom pods,
    2.5 cm piece stick cinnamon,
    4–5 wild long peppers or
    10 whole black peppercorns

1 red onion, chopped

2 cloves garlic, finely chopped

4 cm piece fresh ginger, peeled and
    mashed

2.5 ml chilli powder

5 ml ground coriander

5 ml ground cumin

1 ml turmeric

30 ml tomato purée

2 tomatoes, chopped

30 ml thick Greek yoghurt

1 green chilli, finely chopped

700 g lamb mince

250 g frozen or fresh peas

2.5 ml garam masala (see p. 171)

Sea salt and freshly milled black pepper

1 bunch fresh coriander leaves

4 free-range eggs, hard-boiled

Heat the ghee in a large skillet. Add the whole garam masala spices and when they begin to splutter, add the onion and sauté until brown – this should take about 5 minutes.

Add the garlic and ginger and continue frying for a further few minutes.

Add the chilli powder, ground coriander, cumin and turmeric. Incorporate and sauté for 10 minutes, stirring constantly. If the masala begins to stick to the bottom, add a few splashes of water to deglaze the pan.

Add the tomato purée and fresh tomatoes. Mix well, then add the Greek yoghurt. Sauté for a few minutes. Lower the heat and simmer for 5–8 minutes until the oil begins to appear through the masala. Turn up the heat again and add the green chilli and the lamb mince. Mix well, breaking up any lumps with a wooden spoon.

Once the meat has browned evenly, add about 125 ml water and allow to simmer for about 20 minutes. Add the peas and finally the garam masala powder and season to taste. Cook for a few minutes until the peas have cooked through. The consistency of the dish should be moist but without any liquid or sauce.

Sprinkle with coriander leaves, cut the hard-boiled eggs in half and spread over the meat.

Serve this with pita bread, rotis or parathas.

 Serves 4

 Something different, Tannat or Malbec

COOK'S NOTE

I love warming the pita bread – wrap tightly in some wet parchment paper and nuke it in the microwave for a few seconds. Then spread with some ghee sprinkled with a few chilli flakes.

Nina Timm's Lip-smacking Lamb Ribs

Nina's website – www.my-easy-cooking.com – is a find of fine food steered by budget. Her style is a blend of traditional, heritage food and cutting-edge dishes, and it is so, so delicious.

She says: 'I grew up in Ceres and my family had a farm, so slaughtering a sheep every month was a ritual that to this day is a vivid and precious memory to me. I remember *afval* (tripe) days, I remember my mom saying that lamb neck makes the best green bean stew and lamb knuckle the best *boerekerrie* (farmer's curry). Those precious lessons and pieces of advice I cherish to this day. Lamb ribs, of course, were my favourite and my dad can braai them to perfection. Nothing fancy, no sticky sauces, just the flavour of the meat and time. My dad's secret herbs and spices are simple – salt, pepper and coriander. Maybe sometimes a little splash of Worcestershire sauce.'

Preparing the lamb ribs: If you buy a whole lamb, like we do, prepare the ribs before you freeze them. Cut the ribs into long racks and use a saw or cleaver to crack the ribs at the back. The scoring of the fat is the most important thing and even here I opt for the easy way. I have very sharp knives, but nothing scores fat on lamb and pork belly like a Minora or Lion razor blade. Make sure you cut right through the fat as well as the sinew right underneath the fat. I score 1 cm x 1 cm cubes, so that the spice mix can get right down to the meat. If you can, hang the ribs out for a day or so (this I can only do in winter) or even leave them open in the fridge – it definitely adds flavour.

1 kg lamb ribs

Nina Timm's All-Purpose Spice Mix (see p. 172) or any BBQ spice

1–2 lemons

Use a blade or sharp knife to score the ribs as described above. Season with the spice mix and make sure you rub the spices well into the meat. Allow the meat to rest for at least 1 hour.

Preheat the oven to 180 °C or prepare coals to medium heat.

When roasting in the oven, place the ribs on a roasting rack and tray. Cover with foil and cook until the ribs are tender (this can take a couple of hours), then remove the foil and roast until crispy and golden brown. When you can pull a little bone from the meat, you know it is done.

When preparing them over coals, place the ribs in a folding grid and grill over medium to low coals while turning frequently, or you can make what they call in Namibia *skuinsrib* or *staanrib*. This simply means that the grid with the meat stands next to the fire at an angle. This way the fat drips off and you have a crispier result.

Just before you remove the ribs from the grid or the oven, squeeze over some lemon juice and roast for another minute on each side.

Serve with a salad and fresh farm bread.

Serves 4

 A long cooking time, you'll need a glass of Cape Brandy to revive you

My Cabbage Bredie, in the Style of Louis Leipoldt

As I've mentioned before, C. Louis Leipoldt was very circumspect when describing his recipes. His cabbage bredie from *Kos vir die Kenner* roughly translates to: 'Braise the meat, onions, chillies etc. Slice a head of cabbage very fine and add with pepper and salt. Let it cook slowly. When the meat is soft, add a few potatoes and a nut of butter. Cook until quite dry.' There is no way an average cook can work their way around this vague description.

This is my version.

325 g tight head green cabbage, or a Savoy cabbage if you get lucky

Extra virgin olive oil

1.5–2 kg lamb for stewing, such as neck and ribs

2 onions, wedged (cut each half into 6 wedges like an orange)

3 fat cloves garlic, finely chopped

1 wine cork-size piece fresh ginger, peeled and finely chopped

1–2 bird's-eye chillies, chopped or 1–2.5 ml dried chilli flakes

1 litre lamb stock

3 medium potatoes, peeled and quartered and boiled in salted water

Sea salt and freshly milled white pepper

30 ml finely chopped fresh parsley

Preheat the oven to 170 °C.

Slice the cabbage finely (Leipoldt says '*in rafeltjies*'), removing the hard stem parts, and place in a large bowl. Keep covered with a cloth while you prepare the remainder of the dish.

Using a suitable-size enamelled cast-iron casserole, pour in a thin film of olive oil and allow to heat over medium heat. Brown the lamb pieces, a few at a time, transferring them to a plate as you go. Set aside.

Place the onions in the casserole and allow to get quite golden brown. Do this over low heat and allow time. When done, add the garlic, ginger and chilli and stir-fry for a while.

Return the meat and its juices to the casserole. Add the lamb stock. Make a paper cartouche to cover the casserole (I usually use the lid as a guide). Scrunch it up and place on top of the lamb, then cover with the lid. Cook in the oven for 2½ hours.

Remove the casserole from the oven and discard the cartouche. Add the potatoes, and more liquid if you need to, then pile the cabbage on top. Put the lid back on and allow to simmer on the stove for 30–40 minutes until the cabbage is cooked. Test to see that the lamb is tender. Taste and season if necessary.

Add the parsley and stir through before serving.

Serve with steamed basmati rice and a bowl of roasted carrots flavoured with a little honey or dry sherry.

Serves 4

Something to make a statement: Cabernet Franc

Lamb Knuckle and Quince Bredie

Having grown up on a wine farm in Durbanville, we had the usual things growing in the garden – Cape gooseberries, pomegranates, mulberries, figs and, of course, quinces, one of my most beloved fruits.

This is again a reworked version of one of Louis Leipoldt's sketchily described dishes. I felt that he used too much quince, so I cut down the quantity and reconstructed the recipe.

3 kg lamb knuckles, sliced

Sea salt and freshly milled black pepper

Flour (seasoned with sea salt, freshly milled black pepper, sweet smoked paprika, and a pinch each of ground ginger and ground cloves)

Extra virgin olive oil

4 onions, finely chopped

3 fat cloves garlic, finely chopped

2 large carrots, peeled and diced

2 sticks celery, diced

3 bird's-eye chillies, finely chopped (leave out the seeds and membranes if you want a milder taste)

100 ml brandy

250 ml fruity dry red wine

3 large quinces, peeled and cut into eighths, seeded and cored and kept in acidulated water to prevent oxidation

1 generous sprig fresh thyme, plus extra for garnishing

4 bay leaves

4 blades mace

30 ml tomato paste

1 litre very hot beef stock

Season the lamb knuckles well with sea salt and freshly milled black pepper. Dip them into the seasoned flour and shake off the excess. Slow-fry them in a little oil in a large pan over medium heat until they are well browned on the outside. Do not do them all at once otherwise the meat will stew rather than brown; rather do them in three batches. When done, transfer the knuckles to an ovenproof casserole.

Wipe out the pan with kitchen paper and pour in a little oil. Slow-fry the onions and garlic until they are just starting to colour. Add the carrots, celery and chillies and cook together for a short while.

Spoon the mixture on top of the lamb. Heat the brandy, ignite it and pour it over the lamb, shaking the casserole until the flames die out. Pour in the red wine and cook over low heat until the wine is almost completely reduced.

Preheat the oven to 180 °C.

Drain the quinces and place them on top of the lamb. Tuck in the thyme, bay leaves and mace. Mix the tomato paste with the beef stock and pour into the casserole. Bring to the boil, cover with a paper cartouche and the lid of the casserole and transfer to the oven for 2–3 hours until the lamb is tender.

Remove from the oven and season to taste. A good thing is to leave it overnight at this point for the flavours to mature. If you are not able to, cook for a further 30 minutes or until the meat is very tender and then stir the quinces gently through the meat.

If you are able to keep it overnight, the next day remove any of the solidified fat that has risen to the top, add a little more stock if necessary and reheat gently over a heat diffuser for about 30 minutes.

Garnish with small sprigs of thyme and serve with plain steamed basmati rice and a green vegetable.

Serves 6

 A bold, beautifully oaked Chardonnay, full of oomph

Waterblommetjiebredie

This recipe is a great tradition in the Cape where waterblommetjies (*Aponogeton distachyos*), also known as *wateruintjies*, fill the ponds and dams in winter and spring with pretty white snowdrop-like, strongly scented flowers. Louis Leipoldt, in his book on Cape cookery, refers to them in English as water hawthorn, and Myrna Robins as water hyacinth.

It is important that the flowers be just opening with the calyces still bright green. To prepare them, remove any of the black centres of the flowers. They need to be soaked in lots of salted water and then rinsed through well in a couple of basins of freshly drawn water.

I have found it best to use a combination of thick rib – which adds a little flavourful fat to the dish – and lean shoulder. Many of the old Cape recipes advocate using 'a bit of sheep's tail to add a bit of fat', and others recommend a 'nice fat leg of lamb'.

30 ml sunflower oil (or more if you need it)

6 medium onions, finely sliced

3 small green chillies, seeded and chopped

6 fat cloves garlic, chopped

3 fat slices fresh ginger, peeled

3 kg lamb (use 1 kg thick rib with bones and 2 kg deboned shoulder), cut into pieces

Sea salt and freshly milled black pepper

6 whole allspice

4 whole cloves

½ nutmeg, freshly grated

250 ml red wine

1 litre good-quality beef stock or demi-glace

2 handfuls wild sorrel or 45 ml lemon juice or tamarind juice

2 kg waterblommetjies, prepared as noted above

1 kg medium potatoes, peeled and quartered

15 ml light brown sugar

Heat the oil in an enamelled cast-iron casserole with a tight-fitting lid and gently fry the onions. As they start turning golden, add the chillies, garlic and ginger and continue frying until golden. Remove and drain on kitchen paper.

In the same casserole, brown the meat in batches over high heat. Transfer the browned meat to a plate.

Pour off any excess oil from the casserole and wipe out with kitchen paper.

Return the meat (with any juices which may have collected on the plate) to the casserole along with the onion mixture. Season well with sea salt and freshly milled black pepper and add the allspice berries, cloves and nutmeg. Pour in the wine and stock and braise either on the stove or in a 180 °C oven for 1½ hours.

It is a good idea to cool the dish at this stage and refrigerate overnight to allow the flavours to mature. If you don't have the time, continue with the recipe.

The following day, reheat the casserole gently.

Place the sorrel on top or add the lemon juice or tamarind juice, then the waterblommetjies and finally the potatoes. Sprinkle over the sugar and spoon over some of the sauce. Steam, simmering gently, for a further 1½ hours either on the stove or in a 180 °C oven.

When ready to serve, stir through gently and serve with steamed white rice and wedges of lemon.

Serves 12

 Good fatty lamb, needs good fatty wine – a truly bold Shiraz

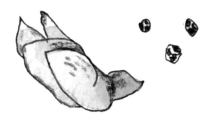

Back Bacon with Plums

I created this dish for a wine product that was exported to Denmark. When plums are in season, they add a lovely acidity to the dish. The bacon you will have to buy from a kind butcher, who can give you a tranche rather than slices.

1 piece back bacon, skin off, weighing about 750 g

Sea salt and freshly milled black pepper

6 ripe blood plums, halved and pips removed

50 g dried cranberries or raisins

250 ml good red wine

30 ml demerara or muscovado sugar

30 ml extra virgin olive oil

4 fat cloves garlic, finely chopped

250 ml verjuice

4 bay leaves

6 whole star anise

2 cinnamon quills

FOR FINISHING THE SAUCE

30 ml quince, redcurrant, apple or berry jelly

Score the fat of the bacon in a diamond pattern. Season well with sea salt and freshly milled black pepper. Take care with the salt as the pork might be sufficiently salty. Place the bacon into a deep ovenproof casserole.

Arrange the plums around the bacon, along with the cranberries or raisins.

Mix the remaining ingredients together in a small bowl and then pour over the bacon. Allow to marinate for at least 2 hours.

Preheat the oven to 200 °C. When ready, place the covered casserole in the oven and cook for 30 minutes. Remove the lid and cook for a further 25 minutes. Check for doneness. Remove from the oven and transfer the bacon to a plate to stand for about 5 minutes to rest.

Meanwhile, remove the bay leaves, star anise and cinnamon from the sauce left in the casserole. Place the casserole over medium heat and mash the plums into the sauce to give it a chunky texture. Add the jelly, squish it down to melt it and then shake the casserole vigorously to create an emulsion – you'll find it absorbs any oil or bacon fat.

Cut the bacon into rough strips and place in the sauce, spooning a little of it over the top.

Serve it in the casserole, with steamed potatoes and a green vegetable such as long-stemmed broccoli or thin 'French' beans.

Serves 4

From Calitzdorp, a red made from Douro varieties

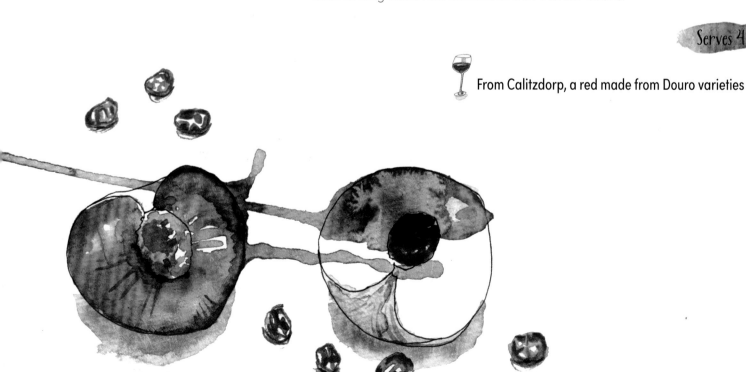

Lager-baked Gammon

This has to be one of the most tender gammons I have ever cooked. I always remove the elastic net from the gammon and leave the skin on to protect it. The skin is removed after baking, before the gammon is glazed. This is great as a hot dish served with real roast potatoes, a green vegetable or two and a smooth apple purée. For us it works wonderfully as a cold meat with lovely fresh sourdough bread, iceberg lettuce and some homemade fruit chutney.

1.5 kg deboned gammon (this is a leg joint)

2 whole cloves

2 bay leaves

340 ml craft lager

45 ml apricot jam

15 ml Dijon mustard

30 ml moskonfyt or honey

Preheat the oven to 170 °C and position the shelf in the middle.

Use a suitable-size dish that will hold the gammon well and place the gammon in it. Use the cloves to fasten the bay leaves to the surface of the gammon (you will have to prick small holes with a skewer as the skin is very tough).

Pour over the lager and transfer the gammon to the oven, uncovered. Bake for 2½ hours, then check with a skewer to be sure it is cooked. It is done if clear juices run out when the gammon is pierced.

Remove from the oven and raise the temperature to 220 °C. Carefully remove the skin and score the fat on the joint in a diamond pattern.

Mix the jam, mustard and moskonfyt or honey together in a small bowl, and thin it down with a little of the liquid from the baking. Brush the glaze over the meat and return to the oven to brown, brushing with more glaze if necessary.

As soon as it is a gorgeous golden brown, it is ready for serving.

Serves 6

 A Rosé? For sure, Grenache or Pinotage

Refogado of Pork Neck

Portugal is one of my favourite countries and I have been fortunate to travel there quite extensively, tasting their great wines. One of the constant memories is of the black-footed pig (*pata negra*), which is served in a variety of ways.

I have used both Port and Pinotage in the recipe as the link between two great wine countries.

1.5 kg pork neck, skin off, filleted and tied, at room temperature

80 ml extra virgin olive oil

2 onions, coarsely chopped

125 ml Port or local Port-style wine

250 ml hearty red wine such as Pinotage

500 ml stock (I used half chicken, half beef)

16 soft dried apricots

2 bay leaves

Freshly milled black pepper

Kneaded butter (an equal mixture in weight of soft butter and flour, well mixed)

RUB OF BO-KAAP SPICES

10 ml coarse sea salt

5 ml ground cinnamon

5 ml ground fennel

5 ml ground cumin

A good splash extra virgin olive oil

Make the rub first. Using a pestle and mortar, pound the salt to break it up a bit. Mix in the spices and pound again to mix well. Add the olive oil to create a thick paste. Rub it generously all over the meat and set aside for about 30 minutes.

Preheat the oven to 180 °C. Make sure the shelf is in the middle and have ready a large oval enamelled cast-iron casserole.

Heat the oil in the casserole over medium heat and carefully brown the meat on all sides. Hold it vertical and sear off the ends as well. Do not be tempted to use too high a temperature, as the spices will burn. Remove the meat and set aside.

Add the onions to the casserole and cook until they are soft and golden brown. Add the Port and, over high heat, allow it to boil away almost completely. Add the wine and stock and allow it to come to the boil, then simmer for a short while to evaporate the alcohol.

Return the meat and any juices that may have collected. Add the apricots and bay leaves. Cover the casserole with the lid and place in the oven for 30 minutes. Lower the heat to 160 °C and braise for 1–1½ hours until cooked through.

Remove the meat, cover with foil and allow to rest for about 20 minutes. Place the casserole on the stovetop over medium heat and reduce the sauce until well flavoured. Adjust the seasoning with freshly milled black pepper and stir in knobs of the kneaded butter to thicken the sauce.

Remove the ties from the meat, slice thinly and place the slices in the sauce. Cover and allow to heat through for about 10 minutes.

Serve with steamed rice and a green vegetable such as steamed Savoy cabbage.

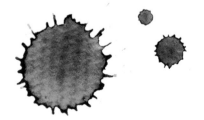

Serves 6

Alvarinho. Albariño. Verdelho

Dine van Zyl's Curried Offal Potjie

Dine van Zyl is a treasure chest of heritage food. This author and television star is famed for penning the first ever book on potjiekos. It was published in 1983 and brought potjiekos out of the history books, and, nearly 40 years later, it remains a popular way of outdoor cooking.

Dine says: 'Potjiekos is pronounced poi-key-koss. Potjie means pot or small pot, and kos means food, so potjiekos means food that is cooked all together in one pot. Potjiekos is cooked out of doors, over the coals, in a black cast-iron pot. This could be a three-legged pot or one with a flat base. Cook potjiekos only when you have time. Relax, talk to your friends, look at the stars.

'Potjiekos is an attitude, a state of mind. It is a way of life, truly South African.

'In the South African context, sheep or lamb offal means the head, tripe (stomach) and trotters all simmered together. This can be done in your potjie, on the stovetop or in the oven. Only use a cast-iron potjie for this dish if it has been well sealed, else the vinegar will turn your offal black and give it a metallic taste. If in doubt, rather use an enamel pot.'

1 complete mutton offal (sheep's head, tripe and trotters), cleaned

250 ml peeled and cubed potatoes

Boiling water to cover

250 ml grape vinegar

15 ml sea salt

5 ml black peppercorns

12 baby potatoes

125 ml smooth apricot jam

CURRY MIXTURE

30 ml crushed fresh ginger

5 cardamom seeds, lightly crushed

5 whole star anise

4 pieces cassia

2.5 ml chilli powder

2.5 ml crushed coriander seeds

2.5 ml whole cloves

5 ml cumin seeds

10 ml turmeric

4 fresh bay leaves

Place the offal and potato cubes in a pot. Cover with boiling water, add the vinegar, sea salt and peppercorns, put the lid on and allow to simmer over coals for 2 hours or longer. Alternatively, cook in a preheated oven at 180 °C.

Now sit back and relax and let the potjie do its thing. There is no need to stir the food, or to pay attention to anything at all. Keep your fire going; not only for the atmosphere, but also to ensure you will have enough coals to cook your potjie.

Once the offal is soft, add the unpeeled baby potatoes as well as the apricot jam.

Mix the curry ingredients in a small bowl and stir the mixture into the potjie. Cover with the lid and allow to simmer. After about 30 minutes, lift the lid.

Use a long-handled spoon to dish up and serve with stampkoring and stewed dried fruit.

~ Serves 6 or 4 hungry souls who

~ haven't had offal in a long time

 A white Jerepigo – lots before, during and after

Desserts

Of course. Who could ever contemplate not serving a
dessert at the end of a family meal? Sometimes after
a main course, we serve cheese. And then a tiny little
sweetness to finish. All sorts of traditional dishes like
pancakes, galettes and tarts can be found here, as well as
the National Treasure – Malva Pudding.

Prickly Pear Pavlova with Rose Petals and Pomegranate Syrup

Prickly pears were very much a part of my childhood, as most farm houses had a cactus in the garden somewhere, like a pile of green dinner plates balanced on top of each other with the pears around the edges.

4 extra-large or jumbo
free-range egg whites

A pinch of fine salt

1 ml cream of tartar

250 g castor sugar, plus
extra for sweetening
the cream

15 ml cornflour

15 ml white wine vinegar

750 ml fresh cream

5 ml vanilla extract

6 ripe prickly pears
(these come in white,
yellow or red)

Pomegranate syrup

2 large open roses (use
yellow roses for white
prickly pears, orange
roses for yellow prickly
pears and pink roses
for red prickly pears)

Preheat the oven to 160 °C. Prepare two baking trays by lining them with non-stick baking paper. Mark out a rectangle on each with a pencil, about 22 cm x 8 cm.

You will need an electric mixer for this recipe. Also, weigh the mixer's bowl – you will need this for later.

Tip the egg whites into the bowl of your mixer. Add the salt and cream of tartar. Start whisking and continue until you have soft peaks. Now add the castor sugar in 50 g increments and continue to whisk well after each addition. When you have added all the sugar, beat well for a while to ensure that all the sugar has dissolved. Add the cornflour and the vinegar and give it a good whisk again. The meringue will now stand up in stiff peaks when you lift out the beater.

Now, having weighed your mixing bowl, you can weigh again so that you have the weight of your mixture which you then divide in two, each portion going on one of the prepared baking trays. Using a spatula, spread the mixture to the edges of your marked-out rectangle, ensuring even thickness throughout.

Place the trays in the oven and turn down the temperature to 140 °C. Bake for 40 minutes, plus another 5 minutes if you feel it necessary. The interior of the meringue will still be soft. Switch off the oven, and wedge open the door using a wooden spoon.

When cold, the two meringues can be kept, wrapped in aluminium foil, until required.

Whip the cream for the filling, sweeten it slightly with castor sugar and add the vanilla extract. Keep half in a separate bowl for the top of the dessert.

Place the one meringue layer on your serving dish of choice. Chop half the prickly pears into chunks and add them to one half of the cream and spread onto the meringue layer. Place the other meringue layer on top and decorate with the remaining cream (to the edges) and the remainder of the prickly pears cut into slices. Dribble over pomegranate syrup and sprinkle over the rose petals, then serve.

Serves 8

Gabriel Boudier Créme de Cassis

How to work with Phyllo Pastry

Phyllo pastry, sometimes spelled filo, is originally of Greek origin and is made with the use of special machinery. It is purchased frozen from your supermarket freezers.

THIS IS THE BEST WAY TO WORK WITH PHYLLO:

- Before you work with the pastry it is best to thaw it overnight in the refrigerator.

- When you are ready to work with it, have all your items ready: a clean wet tea towel to prevent the pastry from drying out; a pastry brush and a bowl of clarified butter; a pastry board; and a baking tray, well greased with melted butter or sprayed with non-stick cooking spray.

- Remove the pastry from the packaging, unroll and immediately cover with the wet tea towel. Carefully remove one sheet of the pastry. Don't worry about tearing, you can fix that easily. Immediately re-cover the remaining pastry with the wet tea towel. Brush the sheet with melted butter and repeat the process until you have used four sheets, one on top of the other.

- Brush the top sheet liberally with butter. Cut into the desired shapes, folding over a seam to prevent the sheets from coming apart.

- Bake according to the recipe until the phyllo is light golden brown and flaky.

- Fill with Crème Pâtissière (see opposite) and fruit, and dust with icing sugar.

- You can sprinkle chopped nuts, such as almonds or pistachios, and castor sugar in between the layers of phyllo before baking.

Crème Pâtissière

**This is a classical pastry cream, so easy to master and so good with desserts.
It's used in various French pastries and as a filling for pancakes.**

6 free-range egg yolks

125 g castor sugar

60 g cake flour

5 ml vanilla extract

500 ml milk

15 g butter

250 ml whipped cream

Cream the yolks and castor sugar in a bowl. Add the flour and the vanilla and beat to a smooth paste.

Place the milk in a saucepan and bring to the boil. Remove from the heat and pour half the milk into the egg mixture, whisking all the while until smooth.

Whisk in the remainder of the milk. Return the mixture to the saucepan and bring to the boil, whisking continuously, until thickened.

Cook, whisking all the while, over medium to low heat for a further 2 minutes to cook the flour. Stir in the butter.

Pour into a bowl, place some buttered greaseproof paper or plastic wrap directly on the surface and refrigerate overnight.

The next day, beat the crème pâtissière with an electric whisk. Beat in a spoonful of whipped cream to 'loosen' the mixture, and then fold in the remainder.

Use as required. It will keep in the refrigerator for a day or so. Just beat well before using.

Makes about 1 litre

Anina Meyer's South African Pannekoek (Pancakes)

Anina Meyer has been a friend for a number of years. No sooner had we moved to Johannesburg in 2018, than she and her family moved to Cape Town. Anina is an amateur turned pro – recipe developer, blogger, food stylist, photographer, cook, sometimes baker and entertainer. She says: 'Yes, despite what you might think, I have no formal culinary background, and quickly had to learn the ropes when I jumped head first into the family Cake Shop many years ago. Menu development and catering was the order of the day. Once I was gifted my first DSLR camera, I went to Google and YouTube school and learned all about food photography and styling – one of my many passions!

'This is an easy one-bowl *pannekoek* that takes no effort at all and is one of our family's best-loved recipes. I don't think it's possible to count how many times over we have used this recipe in the last three decades. From my early childhood, I remember the fun of church bazaars and school fêtes, where the waft of cinnamon sugar literally pulls you towards the stand for a tray of freshly baked *pannekoek*. This South African *pannekoek* is THAT kind of recipe. Therefore, this batter is great to make in bulk when you need to feed a whole army. With a pinch of nostalgia added for good measure ... The South African *pannekoek* way is with plenty of cinnamon sugar, melted into the rolled-up pancake with a dash of fresh lemon juice.'

2 large free-range eggs

750 ml water

5 ml fresh lemon juice

10 ml baking powder

500 ml cake flour

125 ml sunflower oil

FOR SERVING

Castor sugar, flavoured with ground cinnamon

Lemon wedges

In a large mixing bowl, combine the eggs, water, lemon juice, baking powder, flour and oil. Mix with an electric hand-mixer until combined. (I use a normal whisk and I never get any lumps.)

Heat a non-stick pan and add a ladleful of batter. Tilt the pan when you pour in the batter to spread it out all over the bottom. Allow to cook until little bubbles form on top and the sides are easily liftable.

Flip over and allow to cook on the other side.

Serve with cinnamon sugar and a sprinkle of lemon juice.

Makes 10–15 (depending on the size of your pan)

 A glass of Van der Hum

Prue Leith's Normandy Tart

In the 1980s, I met Prue Leith, a South African who has made more than a name for herself in the UK.

She once made us the most fabulous tart with pears. I lost the recipe in a move and was really sad as it was such a fabulous dessert. It's great with pears in summer and makes a perfect winter dessert using apples.

I wrote to her recently and she sent me a copy of the recipe that she had modernised using a food processor to make the pastry.

PASTRY

250 g cake flour

150 g butter

1 free-range egg

A pinch of sea salt

60 g castor sugar

ALMOND FILLING

200 g butter

200 g castor sugar

200 g ground almonds

2 free-range eggs

2 extra yolks

15 ml Calvados, kirsch, or whatever you like

A few drops of almond essence

TOPPING

3–5 eating apples, depending on size

½ jar (200 ml) smooth apricot jam, warmed with a tablespoon of water to a thick syrup

Preheat the oven to 200 °C, and put a metal tray in it to heat.

To make the pastry, whizz everything together in a food processor until the mixture forms a ball. Roll out between two sheets of plastic wrap until big enough to line a 25 cm flan ring. Line the flan ring with the pastry and chill for 30 minutes. If the dish is porcelain, bake blind. If metal, don't bother.

To make the filling, whizz everything in the food processor (no need to wash the bowl after the pastry), then spread in the flan.

To make the topping, peel the apples if you like, then core them and cut in half from stalk end to bottom. Slice each half-apple finely, keeping the slices in order. Arrange them on top of the filling.

Set the flan on the heated tray in the middle of the hot oven and bake for 15 minutes.

Remove the flan from the oven and brush all over with the hot jam. Turn the oven down to 180 °C and bake for 30 minutes or so until the filling is firm and brown.

Remove from the oven and give it another brush with the jam if you think it needs it.

Best served tepid or at room temperature.

Serves 8

 A little glass of French sweetie? Sauternes

COOK'S NOTE

If you make the tart in advance, freeze it and then reheat for 20 minutes at 180 °C, and allow to cool. This will crisp up the pastry again.

Ina Paarman's Tipsy Tart

Were we like the Japanese, Ina Paarman would long ago have been named a Living National Treasure. We have been friends for 40 years and I have been a fan ever since we met, when she showed me how to cook a whole fish wrapped in newspaper over the coals. She has made life in the South African kitchen so much simpler with her easy recipes and great food products.

About the tipsy tart, Ina says: 'A great traditional South African treat to take on a camping trip or for your overseas guests or for granny's birthday. The recipe may seem expensive, but it makes two 24-cm puddings. One is enough to feed eight people. Freeze the other one for later. Do serve with our divine Spiced Brandy Cream!'

SPICED BRANDY CREAM

250 ml fresh cream

A pinch of sea salt

1 ml ground cinnamon

1 ml ground ginger

15 ml sugar

5 ml powdered gelatine

15 ml brandy

PUDDING

5 ml bicarbonate of soda

250 g pitted dates, diced

180 ml boiling water

250 g butter, at room temperature

3 extra-large free-range eggs, at room temperature

1 x 600 g Ina Paarman's Vanilla Cake Mix

250 ml sour cream or crème fraîche

50 g pecan nuts, chopped

SAUCE

125 g sugar

125 ml water

15 ml butter

5 ml vanilla essence

180 ml brandy, sherry or fresh orange juice

Grated orange rind for decorating

Make the spiced brandy cream first so it has enough time to chill. Half-whip the cream with the salt and spices. Add the sugar mixed with gelatine powder and whip until firm. Fold in the brandy. Cover and chill until needed.

To make the pudding, sprinkle the bicarbonate of soda over the dates. Pour the boiling water over them. Set aside and leave to cool.

Preheat the oven to 180 °C and make sure the shelf is in the middle. Butter two 24 cm ovenproof pie dishes.

Ignore the package instructions for the cake mix and follow the method given below.

Cream the butter until soft. Add 1 egg and 15 ml dry cake mix at a time, beating after each addition, until you have used all 3 eggs. Add the sour cream or crème fraîche and beat it in. Add half of the remaining cake mix and all of the date mixture. Stir with a spatula until blended. Add the remaining cake mix and fold in.

Divide the mixture evenly between the two pie dishes. Sprinkle over the nuts and bake for 35 minutes.

While the pudding is in the oven, make the sauce. Bring the sugar, water and butter to the boil in a saucepan. Remove from the heat and stir in the vanilla and brandy, sherry or juice. Prick the tops of the puddings as soon as they come out of the oven. Pour the warm sauce over the hot puddings, then set aside to cool.

Serve with the spiced brandy cream and top with grated orange rind.

Each pudding serves 8

 A good glass of fine Cape Brandy, with a dash of water and ice

Malvapoeding

Malva Pudding

I can happily claim responsibility for the resurgence and subsequent popularity of malva pudding. In the late 1970s, I asked my friend Maggie Pepler, who had the original recipe, to come and work at Boschendal Restaurant, for which I was responsible, while our head chef was on holiday. I asked Maggie to teach us how to make this delicious traditional hot pudding and it has appeared on the buffet at Boschendal Restaurant every day for at least 30 years. There are many versions of this recipe, as people have added a variety of other ingredients such as banana, apple and even caramelised condensed milk! This is the benchmark malva pudding recipe written by Maggie.

PUDDING

250 ml cake flour

15 ml bicarbonate of soda

250 ml sugar

1 free-range egg

15 ml apricot jam

15 ml vinegar

15 ml melted butter

250 ml milk

SAUCE

125 ml fresh cream

125 ml milk

250 ml sugar

125 ml hot water

125 g butter

Preheat the oven to 180 °C. Butter an ovenproof glass or ceramic container measuring approximately 30 cm x 20 cm x 5 cm. Do not use an aluminium, enamel or any metal container. Cut a piece of aluminium foil to cover it while the pudding is in the oven, and grease it well with butter on one side.

To make the pudding, sift the flour and bicarbonate of soda into a bowl and stir in the sugar.

In another bowl, beat the egg very well and add the remaining pudding ingredients, one by one, beating well between each addition.

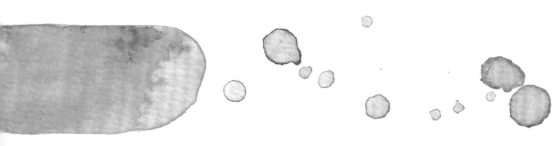

Using a wooden spoon, beat the wet ingredients into the dry ingredients and mix well. Pour the batter into the prepared baking dish, cover with the foil, greased-side down, and bake for 45 minutes until well risen and brown. Bake for a further 5 minutes without the foil if not sufficiently brown. (If not sufficiently baked, the dessert will not take up all the sauce, making it stodgy inside.)

When the pudding is almost done, heat all the ingredients for the sauce, ensuring that you melt all the sugar and butter.

When the pudding is done, remove from the oven, take off the foil and pour over the sauce. The pudding will take up all the sauce.

Serve hot, warm or at room temperature, though warm is best, with a little thin cream.

Serves 6

I think of Sherry, a lovely sweet Spanish Sherry

Nectarine and Cherry Crumble

by Jamie Schler at www.lifesafeast.net

I have known Jamie Schler for some years. She is a brilliant food writer and recipe designer, and an excellent photographer, cookbook author and hotelier with her husband, Jean-Pierre Dagneaux. Jamie is an American living in France. She and JP own the Hotel Diderot in Chinon in the Loire Valley. Her dishes often appear on my website. Do visit Jamie's website for real food inspiration.

RECIPE NOTES

- You'll need 500 g cherries, pitted and halved, and 4–6 nectarines, depending on size, to make up the 6 cups prepared fruit. If using frozen fruit, it does not need to be thawed.

- Replace the orange juice with rum or Amaretto or another liqueur, or even a splash of lemon juice; add cinnamon, ginger or cardamom; use any combination of fruit that you love.

- Cut back the cornflour, if you like. I don't add any when making simple apple or nectarine crumbles, but add it in when baking with berries, cherries or strawberries.

- The combination of nectarines and cherries is a particular favourite – pure pleasure.

FRUIT FILLING

6 x 250 ml fruit (half nectarines, pitted and cubed, and half pitted cherries – see note opposite)

50 g sugar (more if the fruit is very tart or lacks sweetness)

30 ml cornflour

2.5 ml ground cinnamon (optional)

45 ml freshly squeezed orange juice

CRUMBLE TOPPING

130 g cake flour

A pinch of sea salt

2.5 ml ground cinnamon

2.5 ml baking powder

50 g white sugar

55 g light brown sugar

115 g cold butter, cubed

125 ml slivered almonds (optional, but better)

To make the fruit filling, place the prepared fruit in a large mixing bowl. Sprinkle the sugar, cornflour and cinnamon (if using) over the fruit and toss until all the ingredients are well distributed and the cornflour lightly covers all the fruit. I found that the easiest method was simply pushing up my sleeves and using my hands. Stir in the orange juice.

To make the crumble topping, combine all the ingredients, except the butter and almonds, in a large mixing bowl. Toss until well combined. Add the cubes of cold butter and, using your fingertips, rub or work the butter into the dry ingredients until the butter is evenly distributed, there are no more chunks of butter, and the mixture resembles rough sand or crumbs. Toss lightly with the slivered almonds (if using). (If the crumble clumps because of the butter, simply refrigerate it until firm then break it into small chunks and crumble over the fruit.)

Preheat the oven to 190 °C. Place 6–7 individual ramekins on a baking tray and set aside.

Divide the fruit filling evenly among the waiting ramekins. Pour any liquid remaining in the bowl evenly over the divided fruit.

Divide the crumble mixture evenly between the ramekins, spooning it generously on top of the fruit to the edges of the ramekins, making sure that none of the fruit is exposed. Gently press the crumble topping down onto the fruit.

Place the ramekins on the baking tray and bake for 35–40 minutes until the crumble puffs up and turns a deep golden and the fruit bubbles up around the edges of the crumble.

Remove from the oven and allow to cool for a short while before eating. The fruit filling will be too hot to eat straight from the oven.

Serves 6–7

Jamie lives in the Loire Valley in Chinon.
A sweet Chenin Blanc from there?

Gebakte Appels

Baked Apples

Baked apples were such a Sunday lunch tradition, when a large enamel dish was brought to the table and the room was perfumed with apple, honey and spices. Talking of spices, it's not a bad idea to remove the cloves before you start eating – biting on one of those is not a pleasant experience. Cream from our Jersey cows, ice-cold from the refrigerator, was all that was needed to finish this off perfectly.

Butter for baking dish and the apples

6 large cooking apples, such as
    Granny Smith or Golden Delicious

12 whole cloves

Juice of 1 lemon

6 large dates, pitted

3 dried figs

90 ml raisins or sultanas

90 ml chopped almonds

90 ml honey

Water or apple juice for baking

Very cold pouring cream for serving

Preheat the oven to 140 °C. Have ready a well-buttered baking dish large enough to hold all the whole apples.

Peel the skin off the top of the apples and remove the core. Make a slit down each side of the apple. Insert two cloves into the side of each apple. Place in the baking dish, squeeze over the lemon juice and set aside while preparing the filling.

Chop together the fruit and nuts. Stuff into the cored apples and spoon the honey and a pat of butter onto each apple.

Pour a little water or apple juice around the apples and bake until soft and cooked through. Check after 20 minutes.

Serve with pouring cream.

Serves 6

In our house, this was always consumed with sweet Sherry

Lizet Hartley's Rooibos-Poached Pear Mille-feuille with Diplomat Cream

Lizet is the sort of cook we all wish we could be. She produces the most mouthwatering dishes on her website Melkkos & Merlot. I have been a long-time fan and she kindly lets me use her recipes with my wine writing.

4 small Forelle pears, peeled
1 packet store-bought phyllo pastry
Icing sugar for dusting

POACHING LIQUID

2 rooibos teabags
500 ml water
Grated rind of 1 orange
2 cinnamon quills
80 ml sugar
60 ml honey
4 whole cloves
30 ml freshly squeezed lemon juice
30 ml brandy

DIPLOMAT CREAM

3 jumbo free-range egg yolks
80 ml sugar
A pinch of sea salt
30 ml cornflour
250 ml milk
5 ml vanilla bean paste
15 ml cubed cold butter
60 ml cold whipping cream
5 ml castor sugar

To poach the pears, add all the poaching liquid ingredients, except the brandy, to a saucepan. Simmer for a minute or two, stirring to ensure the sugar is dissolved, then remove the teabags. Pop in the peeled pears and simmer until the fruit is soft. Remove the pears from the liquid and set aside.

Strain out the orange rind and whole spices, return the liquid to the saucepan and turn up the heat. Boil the poaching liquid until it is reduced to a syrupy consistency. Add the brandy for the final minute of cooking.

Remove the syrup from the heat and allow to cool to room temperature.

Slice the pears and submerge them in the syrup for at least 1 hour. (The steps above can be done the day before and the syrupy pears kept in the refrigerator until needed.)

To make the diplomat cream, use an electric hand-held whisk to mix together the egg yolks, sugar, salt and cornflour until light and pale yellow.

Heat the milk in a heavy-bottomed saucepan until just below boiling point. Pour the milk into the egg mixture, whisking as you go to prevent scrambling the eggs. Return the mixture to the saucepan, place over gentle heat and use a balloon whisk to stir as it thickens. It takes 2–3 minutes for the mixture to cook and thicken – don't walk away from it, it turns quickly!

Once thick, stir in the vanilla paste. Remove from the heat and whisk in the butter. If you took great care, the pastry cream should be smooth and silky at this point. If it's not, simply push it through a sieve.

Cover with plastic wrap (make sure it's in direct contact with the surface of the pastry cream) and refrigerate for at least 5 hours. (The steps above can be done the day before and the pastry cream kept in the refrigerator until needed.)

To turn the classic pastry cream into diplomat cream, simply whip the whipping cream with the castor sugar until firm. Stir the pastry cream to loosen it a bit, then gently fold the whipped cream into the pastry cream. Return to the refrigerator for 30 minutes to firm up.

In the meantime, preheat the oven to 190 °C. Use scissors to cut the phyllo pastry into squares measuring 7 cm x 7 cm. You will need nine squares per person. Line baking trays with baking paper and place the phyllo squares directly on the baking paper – do not butter the pastry!

Bake the phyllo squares until golden brown – it takes about 7 minutes, but check it after 5 minutes. As these single-layer squares take up a lot of space, you may need to do this in batches, but it's so quick. (The phyllo squares can be baked the day before and stored in an airtight container once cooled.)

To assemble each mille-feuille, place a stack of three phyllo squares on a plate, and top with a dollop of diplomat cream and slices of pear. Repeat with another layer of three pastry sheets, cream and pear slices. Top with three final sheets of phyllo, dust with icing sugar and serve.

Serves 4

A Pear Eau de Vie

Nicky Barber's Peppermint Crisp Ice-cream Parfait

I have known Nicky Barber for some time, and she's an exciting, innovative young woman.
Her website – mydeliciousmonster.com – is well worth a visit.

Nicky says: 'I made my first peppermint crisp tart when I was around eight or nine years old, after being inspired by a school friend during a week of English orals where we could choose any topic and discuss it in front of our class. Cooking demonstrations were allowed, so the no-bake option of a peppermint crisp tart was a good one. So were my devilled eggs – proof that I'd spent far too much time poring over my mom's dinner party recipe books from the eighties and planning my future entertaining endeavours. I opted to use store-bought ice cream as I really didn't feel like making my own, and then the pièce de résistance is the Chocmint Ice Cap, which is super pedestrian but an absolute must!'

2 litres vanilla ice cream

1 packet (200 g) tennis biscuits, crushed (set aside half for the biscuit base)

1 large slab (150 g) Peppermint Crisp, half crushed and half roughly chopped (set aside the roughly chopped portion for decorating)

1 quantity Salted Caramel, see below (set aside half to make sure you have enough to add a few teaspoons to the biscuit base mix and for decorating)

Melted butter

Chocmint Ice Cap

SALTED CARAMEL

250 ml white sugar

60 ml water

30 ml butter

180 ml fresh cream

Maldon sea salt flakes

Start by making the salted caramel. Put the sugar and water in a medium-sized saucepan over medium to low heat and don't stir! You need to allow it to melt completely and begin bubbling until it begins transforming from a clear to amber liquid. When it starts changing, feel free to gently swirl the pan – this will help evenly caramelise the sugar.

Take it off the heat, add the butter and whisk. Once the butter has melted, add the cream and whisk to emulsify everything. Be careful not to burn yourself because when you add the butter and cream the mixture can spit and bubble up. Just keep whisking!

Place the saucepan back on the heat, continuing to whisk for about 1 minute.

Remove from the heat again and add a pinch of Maldon sea salt flakes.

Pour into a heatproof bowl, cover and leave to cool completely. You can place it in the refrigerator to speed things up, but it will become very thick, so you'll need to give it a good mix to loosen it up again before assembling the tart.

To begin assembling the tart, make sure you've lined the long side of a loaf tin with baking paper, allowing a few centimetres of overhang so you can loosen it from the tin before tipping it out onto your serving plate or board. You don't have to do this, but I feel like it's an extra step that might make your life easier when it comes to unmoulding the parfait.

Take the ice cream out of the freezer to soften while you begin with the first layer, which is a dusting of crushed tennis biscuits and peppermint crisp.

Add a layer of ice cream. It doesn't have to be an exact amount, just make sure it's enough to cover the base of the tin once you've smoothed it out with the back of a spoon.

Add another layer of tennis biscuits and peppermint crisp, as well as a generous drizzle of salted caramel. Again, not an exact amount – you do you.

At this point, depending on what ice cream you're using and how hot the weather is, you might need to pop the loaf tin back in the freezer for 15–20 minutes to firm up again.

Continue with another layer of ice cream and repeat until you've either finished the ice cream or almost reached the rim of the loaf tin.

To make the biscuit base, you'll need to combine enough melted butter with the reserved tennis biscuits to moisten them. Add a few teaspoons of salted caramel to the mixture, mix well to combine and then layer on top of the ice cream. Make sure to pack it firmly so you create a sturdy base for the parfait.

Place the loaf tin in the freezer for at least a few hours to firm up completely, or better yet, overnight.

To unmould the parfait, place the tin in a shallow bath of room temperature water for a few seconds so it comes away from the tin more easily. You can check if it's ready by using the wings of the baking paper to gently lift it up without removing it completely. Carefully flip it out onto your serving plate or board, remove the tin and carefully peel away the strip of baking paper. You may want to place the parfait back in the freezer at this point to firm up again until you're ready to decorate.

Decorate the parfait with a dusting of any leftover crushed tennis biscuits and peppermint crisp if you wish, drizzle with reserved salted caramel and scatter over the roughly chopped peppermint crisp. Finish it off with a generous drizzle of Ice Cap and place back in the freezer until ready to slice and serve.

Serves 8–10

A Peppermint Liqueur

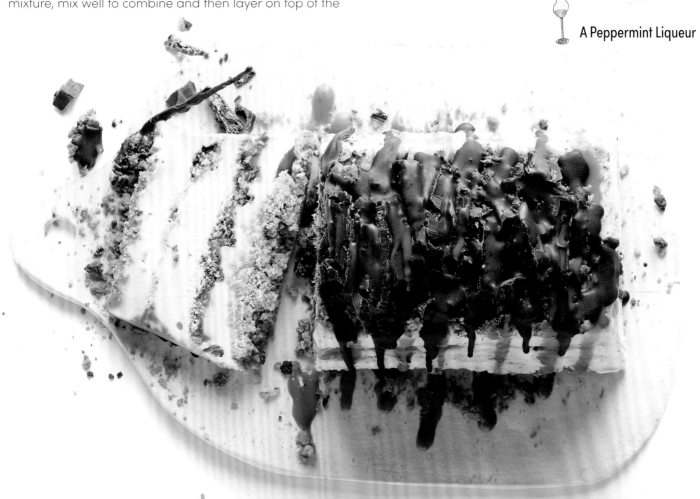

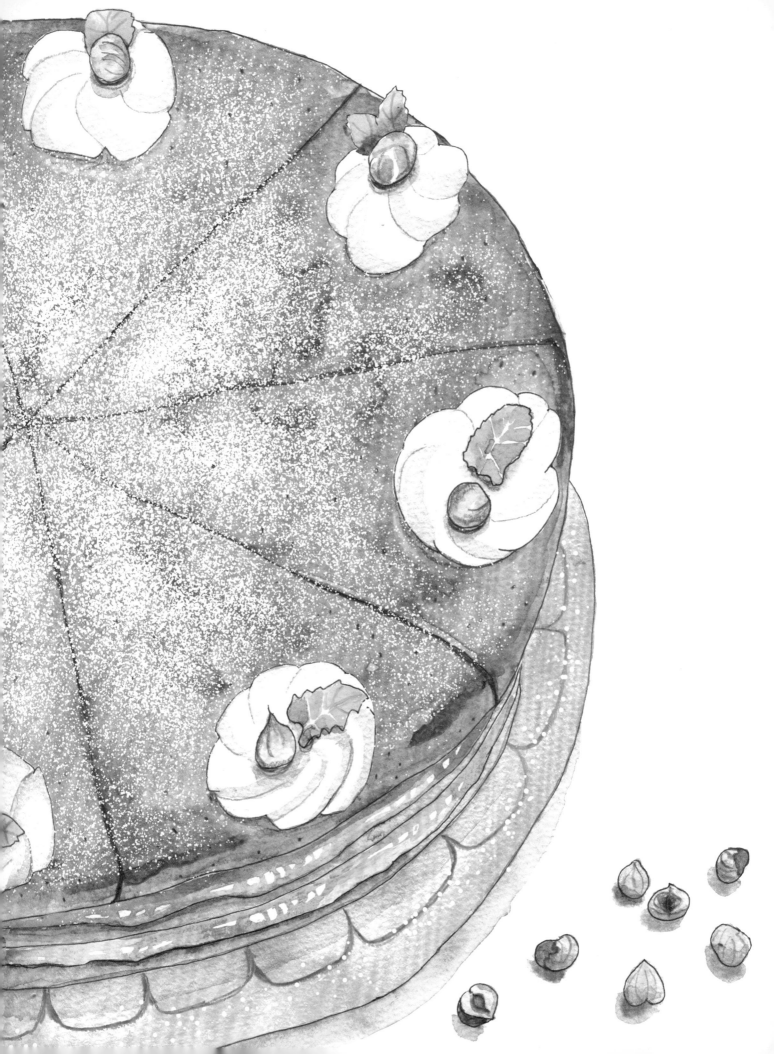

Hazelnut and Apple Galette

My teachers, especially the legendary Rosemary Hume, at Le Cordon Bleu culinary school in London, more than 50 years ago, would be very proud of me for baking this delight.

500 g Golden Delicious or other dessert apples

Grated rind and juice of ½ lemon

Sugar to taste

Icing sugar for dredging

Whipped cream for decorating

8 perfect fresh mint leaves

PASTRY

90 g hazelnuts, plus 8 for decorating

135 g cake flour

A pinch of fine sea salt

97.5 g cold butter, diced

67.5 g castor sugar

To make the filling, peel, core and slice the apples and place in a saucepan. Add the lemon rind and juice and sugar to taste and cook over low heat to break down the fruit. Beat with a wooden spoon and cook down to a purée. Add more sugar if necessary. Set aside and allow to cool.

To make the pastry, preheat the oven to 180 °C. When the oven is ready, toast the hazelnuts for 10–15 minutes until the skins are blistered and the nuts are a light gold in colour. Immediately wrap them in a tea towel, allow to stand for a while, and then rub off the skins. Save the best eight for the garnish and grind the remainder in a food processor until finely crumbed.

Sift the flour with the fine sea salt onto a pastry board or countertop. Make a well in the middle and add the butter and castor sugar. Sprinkle the ground nuts over the flour. Using the tips of your fingers and a light touch, quickly mix the ingredients – don't let the mixture come up beyond the first joint of your fingers. Once it has come together, scrape the pastry off your fingers with a palette knife and then smooth the pastry out with the heel of your hand. Wrap in plastic wrap and refrigerate for at least 30 minutes.

Remove the pastry from the refrigerator, weigh and cut into three equal portions. Roll out into thin circles and place on a baking tray; mark one of them into eight by cutting through to the baking tray. Bake in a preheated oven at 180 °C until cooked and just turning gold around the edges. Remove from the oven and allow to cool.

When cool, place the first layer of pastry on the serving dish. Carefully spread over half the apple mixture, almost to the edges. Repeat with the second layer of pastry and the rest of the filling. Carefully place the eight portions of pastry on top. Dust heavily with icing sugar. Pipe a cream rose on the edge of each slice and decorate it with a hazelnut and a mint leaf. Serve immediately.

Serves 8

 A not-too-little glass of Calvados, with a dollop of mineral water and ice

Rosyntjietert

Raisin Tart

The Cape is well known for its Muscat grapes. Today they are known as 'Hanepoot', which could be a corruption by household or farming staff of the word 'honeypot', which the early British settlers may have called them.
In late summer, when they were very sweet on the vine, they were picked and dried to raisins for use throughout the rest of the year.

Muscat grapes were also used on the Constantia Wine Estate (now Groot Constantia) for the manufacture of Constantia Wine – drunk by the crowned heads of Europe and used by Napoleon in exile on St Helena island. Jane Austen recommended it to her heroines. Groot Constantia Estate in Cape Town today makes a replica of this wine, which it packs in a historic-looking bottle.

1 x 23 cm pie dish lined with unbaked flaky pastry
150 g seedless raisins
80 g sugar
250 ml water
25 ml fresh white breadcrumbs
65 ml chopped almonds
Grated rind of 1 lemon
A grating of nutmeg
A pinch of ground cinnamon
A pinch of ground ginger
A pinch of ground cloves
A pinch of ground allspice
A pinch of fine sea salt
30 ml smooth apricot jam
15 ml cake flour
15 ml lemon juice
5 ml butter
1 free-range egg yolk
30 ml brandy

Preheat the oven to 200 °C and have ready the pie dish lined with the pastry. Scallop the edges of the pastry.

Bring the raisins, sugar and water to the boil in a saucepan. Stir in the breadcrumbs, almonds, lemon rind, spices and apricot jam.

Make a paste from the flour and lemon juice, add a little water and stir the paste into the raisin mixture. Reduce the heat, add the butter and simmer until the mixture has thickened and is cooked through. Remove from the heat and allow to cool slightly.

Beat the egg yolk and the brandy and stir into the raisin mixture. Spoon the mixture into the pastry-lined pie dish and bake for 25 minutes.

Serve with a warm egg custard that has been scented with peach leaves.

Serves 6

 A sweet white wine, well chilled

Afternoon Tea

Not even the smell of frying bacon beats the smell of a bake coming out of the oven. There is a lovely selection here, including traditional fruit cakes for Christmas, a Simnel Cake, and my Sydney friend Roberta Muir's Anzac Biscuits, which Australians and New Zealanders consider theirs by right. For me, waking up to the smell of frying Koeksisters that permeated the house on a Saturday morning, and the smell of the cinnamon syrup into which they are dumped, sizzling and sucking up the spicy sweetness, will remain with me forever.

My Grandmother's Christmas Cake

Based on a recipe my grandmother used for the entirety of my childhood, this cake was usually made on Stir-Up Sunday in November, when the Christmas puddings were also made. I was allowed to stir, clockwise only, 'or else you let the devil in'. The brandy is very important – the cake is fed on it in the weeks leading up to Christmas.

100 g currants

150 g raisins

250 g Orange River or golden sultanas

100 g glacé pineapple, roughly chopped

100 g glacé cherries, halved

100 g candied mixed peel

125 ml KWV brandy, plus more for the weekly soak

125 g butter, at room temperature

130 g cake flour

2.5 ml baking powder

1 ml each sea salt, freshly milled black pepper, ground ginger, ground cloves and ground nutmeg

50 g ground almonds

125 g soft brown sugar

4 free-range eggs, whisked

Grated rind of 1 lemon and 1 orange

50 g whole almonds

45 ml finely chopped preserved ginger

Place the currants, raisins, sultanas, pineapple, cherries and peel in a bowl and pour over the brandy. Cover with plastic wrap and leave overnight.

Place the butter on a shelf in the kitchen so that it is at room temperature in the morning. The cake tin – a 20 cm ring – was lined with a double layer of greaseproof paper (we use silicone paper now and spray with non-stick cooking spray) and also prepared the night before.

In the morning, preheat the oven to 140 °C.

Sift together the flour, baking powder, salt, spices and ground almonds.

Using an electric beater, cream the butter and sugar at slow speed and then beat until light and fluffy. Add the eggs, one at a time, adding a little of the flour mixture each time to prevent curdling. Fold the remainder of the flour mixture into the butter cream and add the soaked fruits, any remaining brandy, the lemon and orange rinds, the whole almonds and the preserved ginger.

Spoon the mixture carefully into the prepared cake tin, smoothing over the surface, and creating a slight hollow in the middle to prevent a raised top. Place the cake into the oven and bake for 1 hour. Cover with a sheet of aluminium foil and bake for a further 30 minutes. Insert a skewer in the middle – if it comes out clean, the cake is cooked. If not, test every 10 minutes until the cake is done. Remove from the oven and allow to cool in the tin.

Once cool, turn out the cake, poke some holes in it and pour over a little brandy. Cover the cake in muslin and store in a cake container. Once a week, take the cake out and pour a little brandy over it.

Ice the cake the day before Christmas or leave it without icing and dust with icing sugar.

Serves 12–15

My Granny's Simnel Cake

Simnel Cake is traditionally baked at Easter and has 11 eggs made from marzipan on top, signifying the 11 Apostles. Judas, having betrayed our Lord shortly before his crucifixion, does not merit an egg.

In our house it was always baked a week or so ahead of Easter so that it had time to mature. While most people use store-bought marzipan, usually made from almond-flavoured apricot kernels, my grandmother used to buy ground almonds in a tin, which you opened with a tin opener, and it went whoosh!

ALMOND PASTE

250 g castor sugar

250 g ground almonds

2 free-range eggs, beaten

5 ml vanilla extract (some like to use almond extract)

CAKE

180 g cake flour

1 ml each grated nutmeg, ground ginger, ground cloves and fine sea salt

180 g butter (don't be remotely tempted to use margarine or vegetable fat)

180 g soft brown or Muscovado sugar

3 extra-large free-range eggs

150 g raisins

150 g golden sultanas

50 g currants

60 g chopped mixed peel

Grated rind of 1 lemon and 1 orange

30 ml smooth apricot jam

1 free-range egg, beaten, for brushing over the cake before grilling

Prepare a 20 cm cake tin by lining it, bottom and sides, with greaseproof or silicone paper.

To make the almond paste, mix the sugar and ground almonds in a large bowl. Add just enough egg to give the paste a soft texture. Flavour with the vanilla extract and knead gently for about a minute. Set aside for a few hours to allow it to firm up (or make it the day before). You will need to roll (on a lightly floured surface) about a third of the weight of the almond paste to make a circle 18 cm in diameter, which will go into the centre of the cake. Set aside the rest for later.

Preheat the oven to 140 °C.

To make the cake mixture, sift together the flour, spices and salt in a bowl.

Cream the butter in the bowl of a food mixer, and then add the sugar and beat together until pale in colour and light in texture. Add the eggs, one at a time, with about a third of the flour mixture – this helps prevent curdling. Add the remainder of the flour mixture, the fruits, mixed peel and grated rinds and mix well. Spoon half the batter into the prepared cake tin. Level it off and then put the circle of marzipan on top. Spoon the rest of the batter on top and smooth over, allowing a bit of a dent in the middle so that the cake ends up with a flat top.

Bake for 1 hour 45 minutes. Insert a metal skewer into the middle – if it comes out clean, the cake is baked. If not, test again after a further 10 minutes. Remove the cake from the oven and cool in the tin for about 15 minutes, then turn out onto a cake rack to cool completely. When the cake is completely cool, remove it from the greaseproof or silicone paper. Set your oven's grill on high.

Heat the apricot jam and brush over the top of the cake. Using half of the remaining marzipan, roll it out into a 20 cm circle and place it carefully on top of the cake. With the remaining marzipan, roll out 11 small egg-shaped balls and place them round the edge. Brush the marzipan and the egg-shaped balls with beaten egg and set in the oven to brown gently, watching all the time, for 1–2 minutes, depending on the heat of your grill. Alternatively, use a blow torch to brown it.

Decorate with little candy or chocolate Easter eggs. And do place a little fluffy chicken on top.

Serves 12–15

Granny's Three-Colour Pound Cake

My grandmother always baked early in the morning. The ingredients all stood out of the refrigerator overnight so that they were at room temperature. I demonstrated this cake on *Expresso* one morning and got a bit enthusiastic with the red food colouring – it was way too brightly coloured, so be careful...

125 g unsalted butter, plus extra for greasing

220 g cake flour

10 ml baking powder

2.5 ml sea salt

250 g white sugar

3 large free-range eggs

5 ml vanilla extract

165 ml buttermilk

37.5 ml cocoa powder

Red food colouring

Preheat the oven to 180 °C. Grease (with the extra butter) a 22 cm loaf tin. Sift in some flour to coat the butter and tap out the excess.

Sift together the flour, baking powder and salt into a bowl.

Using a wooden spoon and a separate bowl, or an electric beater, whip the butter until light and fluffy and then beat in the sugar a little bit at a time. Add the eggs, one by one, with a generous spoon of the flour mixture to prevent curdling. Add the vanilla with the last egg.

Add the remaining flour alternately with the buttermilk. Spoon one-third of the batter into the loaf tin. Divide the remainder into two bowls.

Dissolve the cocoa in a little boiling water and add to one bowl. Stir in well and spoon on top of the vanilla batter.

Colour the remaining batter with the red food colouring and spoon on top of the chocolate batter.

Using a knife in a round and round motion, stir the three batters to make a marbled pattern, but don't stir too much. Bake in the preheated oven for 40–50 minutes, turning the loaf tin after 20 minutes, until a skewer inserted in the middle of the cake comes out clean.

Remove from the oven and place the tin on a cooling rack for 10 minutes. Turn the cake out of the loaf tin and cool completely. The cake can be iced with butter icing or just sprinkled with icing sugar.

With any luck the cake might last for three days, if you can keep your kids away from it!

Serves 12

COOK'S NOTE

You don't have to do the colour layers in the same order as given above. The marbling effect makes it unique each time anyway!

Sue Barber's Carrot Cake

Sue Barber and I have known each other for many years. She is a great cook and her style is quite eclectic as she has lived in Mauritius for many years, where her husband, O'Brian, was a golf professional. Sue made this cake for me for my birthday a couple of years ago. I know that carrot cake is in most people's repertoire, but this one's a goodie. I give it to you as Sue gave it to me.

CAKE

4 free-range eggs

500 ml castor sugar

125 ml sunflower oil

500 ml cake flour

5 ml bicarbonate of soda

10 ml baking powder

10 ml ground cinnamon

5 ml sea salt

500 ml grated carrots

1 tin (432 g) crushed pineapple, drained

250 ml chopped pecans or walnuts

CREAM CHEESE FROSTING

200 g full-fat cream cheese,
   at room temperature

100 g butter, at room temperature

600 g icing sugar, sifted

Grated rind and juice of 1 lemon

Pecan or walnut pieces for decorating

Preheat the oven to 180 °C. Grease a cake tin of your choice (or two tins if you want to make a layer cake) with non-stick cooking spray.

Cream the eggs until light and fluffy, then add the castor sugar slowly. Add the oil.

Sift together the flour, bicarbonate of soda, baking powder, ground cinnamon and salt.

Add the dry ingredients to the egg and sugar mixture and mix well. Then add the grated carrots, pineapple and nuts and mix well again.

Spoon the batter into the prepared cake tin(s) and bake for about 1 hour until a skewer inserted into the middle comes out clean. Baking time will vary depending on the size of the cake tin(s) used, so adjust accordingly. Do not overbake this cake, as the moister it is, the better.

Remove the cake(s) from the oven and allow to cool in the tin(s).

To make the frosting, place the cream cheese, butter and icing sugar in a mixing bowl. Using an electric beater on slow speed, mix until light and fluffy. Add the lemon rind and juice to taste. If the mixture is too soft, add a bit more icing sugar.

Decorate the cooled cake with the frosting and top with the pecan or walnut pieces.

Serves 10

Samantha Linsell's Hummingbird Cake

I have known and loved Sam Linsell for a number of years. Trained at the Hotel School in Johannesburg, she has gone on to make a career for herself in food, food writing and photography. She is a star turn.

Sam says: 'This banana and pineapple hummingbird cake is one of my all-time favourite cakes. It has an incredibly moist crumb and, overall, it's not cloyingly sweet. The cream cheese frosting finishes it off perfectly. This can easily be converted to a carrot cake by replacing 375 ml of the pineapple with grated carrot and the banana with grated apple, or do a combo of some or all of them.'

4 free-range eggs

375 ml white or light brown sugar

250 ml sunflower oil

500 ml cake flour

2.5 ml sea salt

10 ml baking powder

5 ml bicarbonate of soda

5 ml ground cinnamon

1 ml ground cloves

1 ml grated nutmeg

500 ml finely chopped pineapple, tinned or fresh

375 ml finely chopped and slightly mashed banana (about 4 small to medium bananas)

180 ml chopped walnuts

CREAM CHEESE FROSTING

100 g butter, at room temperature

125 g cream cheese

750 ml icing sugar

10 ml lemon juice

A few walnuts for decorating

Preheat the oven to 180 °C. Line two 23 cm round springform cake tins with non-stick baking paper.

In an electric mixer, beat the eggs and sugar until light and fluffy (about 4 minutes). Add the oil and continue beating.

Sift the flour, salt, baking powder, bicarbonate of soda and spices into the mixture and mix briefly to incorporate. Remove the bowl from the mixer.

Fold in the chopped fruit and nuts and evenly divide the batter between the two cake tins. Bake for about 1 hour until firm and a skewer inserted into the middle comes out clean.

Allow the cakes to cool in the tins on a rack before removing and icing.

To make the icing, beat all the ingredients together using an electric mixer until light and fluffy. Ice the cooled cake, using a third of the icing to sandwich the layers together. Finely chop up a few walnuts and scatter over the cake to decorate.

Makes 1 large cake (serves 12–16)

COOK'S NOTES

If the top of the cake is getting too dark but it is not yet baked through, loosely cover it with a piece of aluminium foil and continue to bake until done.

Double the quantity of frosting if you want thicker layers.

Melktert

Milk Tart

Most popular as an accompaniment to morning or afternoon tea or coffee, *melktert* dished with a selection of glacé fruits makes for a classy dessert too.

500 g puff pastry

3 jumbo free-range eggs, separated

50 g cake flour

45 ml cornflour

50 g sugar

600 ml milk

1 cinnamon quill

1 star anise

4 cardamom seeds

5 ml vanilla paste or extract

15 ml butter

Ground cinnamon for dusting

Use the pastry to line a 25 cm pie plate, building up an edge with the offcuts. Using a pastry brush, paint the inside of the pie with a little of the egg white and place in the refrigerator until required.

Mix together the flour, cornflour and all but 15 ml of the sugar. Add a little milk and stir into a paste until smooth. Add the remaining milk, cinnamon, star anise, cardamom seeds and vanilla paste. Pour into a saucepan and bring to the boil, stirring all the while. Add the butter and stir.

Beat the egg yolks and then beat in a little of the hot liquid. Pour this mixture into the rest of the hot milk mixture.

Return to low heat for a minute or so, stirring to cook the egg yolks. Remove from the heat, strain out the whole spices and allow the custard to cool slightly.

Preheat the oven to 230 °C.

Meanwhile, whisk the egg whites until stiff. Add the remaining 15 ml sugar and beat again. Fold into the cooled custard and spoon into the pie crust. Sprinkle lightly with ground cinnamon. Bake in the middle of the oven for about 10 minutes. Reduce the oven temperature to 180 °C and bake for a further 15–20 minutes so that the filling can rise well and be cooked through. When it is golden brown, switch off the oven and allow to stand for a further 5 minutes.

Allow to cool and serve as is or with glacé fruits.

Serves 8–10

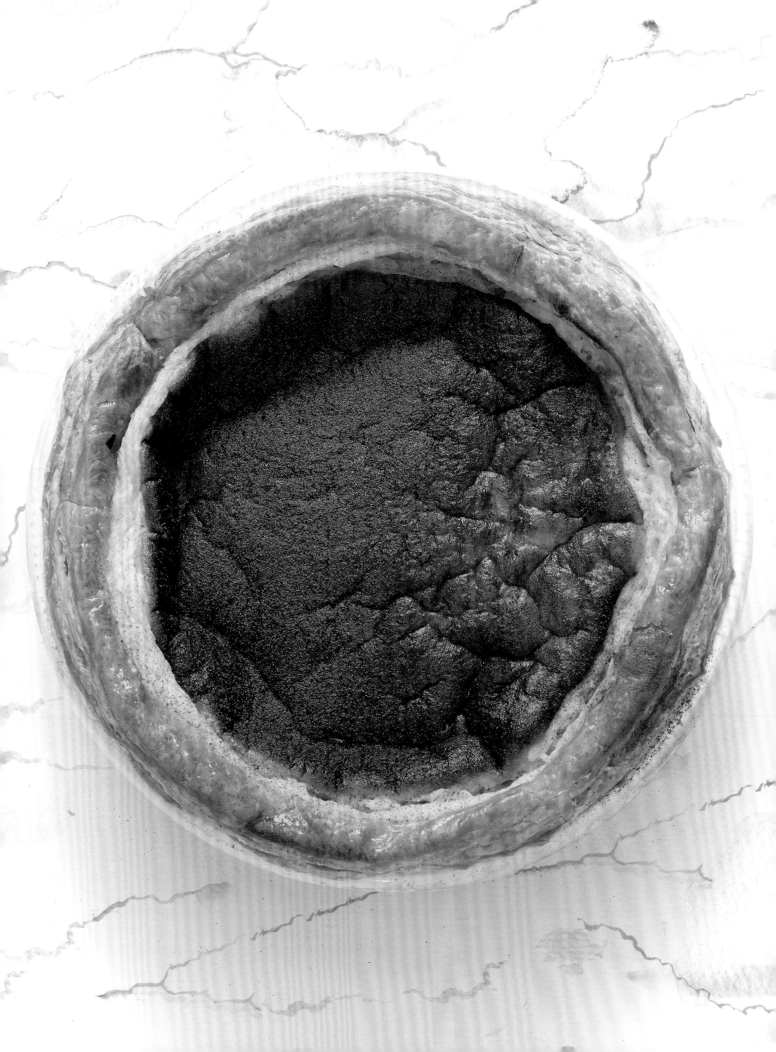

Daphne Enslin's Brandy Snaps

Daphne Enslin, who trained in Scotland, introduced these to the dessert buffet at Boschendal in the late 1970s when we worked there. They were loved by the VIP guests, including Henry Kissinger, who said to me at lunch: 'You keep Nancy busy while I get another brandy snap!'

150 g golden syrup

150 g butter

125 g yellow sugar

45 ml brandy

120 g cake flour sifted with
   5 ml ground ginger

Preheat the oven to 190 °C. Lightly butter two baking trays.

Melt the syrup, butter and sugar together in a saucepan over low heat.

Remove the saucepan from the heat, allow to cool slightly and then add the brandy and the flour mixture. Stir well. Place teaspoon-size dollops well apart on the baking trays to allow room for spreading.

Bake for 6 minutes until golden brown. It's best to bake them in batches to allow enough time to roll each snap before they harden.

Cool for a minute to allow them to firm up slightly. Roll around the handle of a wooden spoon or shape over dariole moulds to form cups.

Use as desired. If you roll them, pipe whipped cream into each end shortly before serving.

Makes about 32

Roberta Muir's Anzac Biscuits

Roberta Muir has been a friend for a number of years. She is university trained, and a cookbook author, food writer and recently retired manager of the Sydney Seafood School. She and her husband, Frans Scheurer, a professional photographer, musician, collector of timepieces and and and, have a passion for good cooking, eating and drinking, and exciting travel in search of all three.

She says: 'A number of foreign friends living in Australia have said that Anzac Day feels more like our national day than Australia Day does. And the legend of the Australian and New Zealand Army Corps, and their battle at Gallipoli on 25 April 1915, is certainly etched deep in the Australian psyche. It's so sacred, in fact, that legislation protects the word "Anzac" and a permit is required to use it. Luckily, applications for "Anzac Biscuits" are usually granted (as mine was), though the Department of Veteran Affairs is strict about following a traditional recipe and frowns on the name Anzac Cookies! So, here's my version of these crisp, chewy biscuits that were, I believe, sent in care packages to the soldiers on the frontline in WWI. When you enjoy these biscuits with a cup of tea, spare a thought for them, and for all the others who have risked their own safety and comfort to protect ours. The story of the Anzac battle at Gallipoli looms large in Australian culture.'

250 ml rolled oats

250 ml cake flour

180 ml castor sugar

180 ml shredded coconut

125 g salted butter

30 ml golden syrup

5 ml bicarbonate of soda

Preheat the oven to 160 °C. Line two baking trays with baking paper.

Combine the oats, flour, castor sugar and coconut in a mixing bowl.

Place the butter and golden syrup in a saucepan over low heat until the butter melts.

Remove the saucepan from the heat and stir in the bicarbonate of soda (it will froth up).

Pour the butter mixture over the oats mixture and stir to combine very well to form a dry but cohesive mixture – add 5–10 ml water if necessary.

Roll tablespoonfuls of the mixture into balls, flatten into discs and place onto the prepared baking trays, about 5 cm apart.

Bake for 15–20 minutes until golden. Remove from the oven and set aside to cool on the trays.

Makes about 24

Hertzogkoekies
Coconut and Apricot Jam Tarts

James Barry Munnik Hertzog was prime minister of the Union of South Africa from 1924 to 1939. Urban legend has it that these tarts were baked in the Bo-Kaap above Cape Town when the women of South Africa were promised the franchise by Hertzog. When the laws were passed, it was only the white women who got the vote. Legend has it that the ladies of the Bo-Kaap then baked another biscuit which had half pink and half brown icing on top, and these were known as *tweegevreetjies* – little two faces!

Sufficient short crust or puff pastry to line 24 patty pans

Smooth apricot jam or apple jelly

3 free-range egg whites

A pinch of sea salt

150 g white sugar

125 g desiccated coconut

5 ml baking powder

Line the patty pans with short crust or puff pastry. Prick with a fork. Put a small spoonful of apricot jam or apple jelly in the middle of each and then chill in the refrigerator until required.

Preheat the oven to 180 °C.

In a clean bowl free of any liquid or fat, whisk the egg whites and the pinch of salt until stiff. Add the sugar slowly, whisking all the while. Fold in the coconut and baking powder with the edge of a metal spoon.

Cover the apricot jam or apple jelly in the tarts generously with the coconut mixture.

Bake in the oven for 15 minutes or a little longer to allow the coconut to brown lightly.

Makes 24 tarts

Koeksisters

Braided Crullers

A fond childhood memory for me was waking up early on a Saturday morning when koeksisters were being made for a church cake sale. The syrup was always made on Friday nights and allowed to get really cold overnight, one of the secrets of the success of koeksisters. Even during use it was surrounded with ice cubes so that the hot koeksisters would suck in the cinnamon and lemon syrup. The oil also could not be too hot (180 °C), otherwise the koeksisters would be dark and hard on the outside and not properly cooked on the inside. Koeksisters were originally from Batavia and are generally plaited. Koesisters (also known as a bollas) are often made with mashed potato, and are cooked in an oblong shape (not plaited) and served rolled in coconut.

SYRUP

1 kg white sugar

500 ml water

4 pieces stick cinnamon, about 4 cm in length

6 whole cloves

6 whole allspice

2 thumb-size pieces fresh green ginger, well bruised with a rolling pin

3 strips lemon peel, 2 cm wide and 4 cm long

30 ml lemon juice

A pinch of sea salt

A knife point of cream of tartar

5 ml glycerine – add just before dipping to give the koeksisters a shiny coat.

KOEKSISTERS

500 g cake flour

20 ml baking powder

5 ml ground mixed spice

2.5 ml sea salt

60 g butter, frozen and cut into tiny squares

250 ml milk

125 ml buttermilk

Sunflower oil for deep-frying

The day before, prepare the syrup. Combine all the ingredients, except the glycerine, in a saucepan and heat gently while dissolving the sugar. When the sugar has dissolved, bring the mixture to the boil and boil for 5 minutes. Set aside and allow to cool. Leave the spices and peel in the syrup and, when sufficiently cold, pour into a glass bowl and place in the refrigerator overnight. Shortly before use, it can be placed in the freezer to get it really cold.

Now prepare the koeksister dough. Sift the flour, baking powder, mixed spice and salt into the bowl of a food processor. Add the butter and pulse until the mixture resembles a coarse meal. Add the milk and buttermilk and pulse until the ingredients are combined. Turn out onto a floured board and knead gently until the mixture forms a soft dough.

Divide the mixture in two and place in separate bowls. Cover with a damp tea towel and set aside for 30 minutes to allow it to rest.

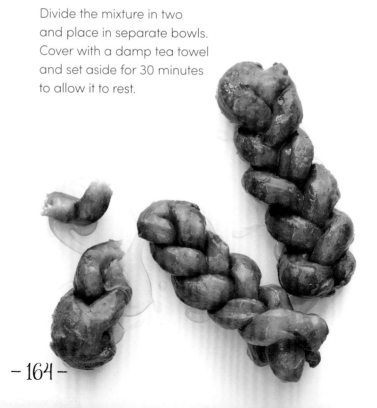

When you are ready to make the koeksisters, have the following items set out: one baking tray covered with greaseproof paper, another baking tray lined with absorbent kitchen paper, a third tray containing a cake rack on which to drain the koeksisters once they have been dipped into the syrup, and a large bowl filled with ice to hold the bowl with the strained syrup. Also have ready two slotted spoons: one for lifting the koeksisters out of the hot oil and another for putting them into and removing them from the syrup.

Pat one of the balls of dough out on a floured board into a rectangular shape. Using a floured rolling pin, roll it out into a rectangle measuring 20 cm long x 10 cm wide x about 1 cm thick. Cut into four across the length so that you end up with rectangles measuring 5 cm x 10 cm. (This will give you four koeksisters from each ball of dough.) Cut each one into three strips, leaving them joined across the top. Plait them, seal the ends with water and tuck them underneath. Place them on the baking tray with the greaseproof paper and cover with the damp tea towel while you repeat the process with the other ball of dough.

In a deep, heavy-bottomed saucepan, heat the oil to 180 °C (check with a food thermometer) and then deep-fry the koeksisters in batches of four at a time, turning them with the slotted spoon to brown them evenly on both sides.

Remove from the oil and drain on the tray with the kitchen paper for a short while. While they are still hot, drop them into the ice-cold syrup for about a minute. When ready, remove them with the other slotted spoon, drain a moment and place them on the cake rack. Continue with this process until all the koeksisters have been fried and dipped in the syrup.

Serve them warm (when they are at their best) or at room temperature.

Makes 8 koeksisters

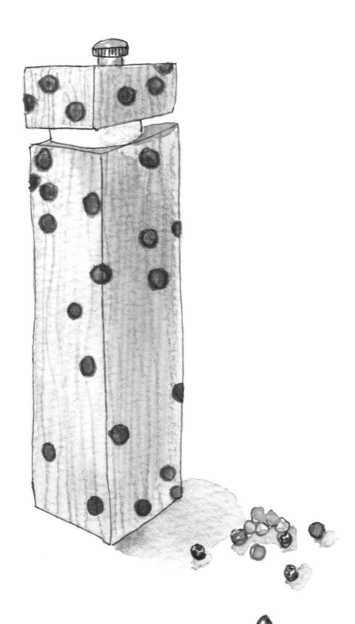

Bits and Bobs

In a book like this there are always recipes that we aren't sure quite where they belong. Loved as they are, they have a chapter of their own at the end.

Romesco Sauce

This is a sauce of Spanish origin. It's great on meat and chicken off the braai, and excellent with fish, slices of grilled aubergine or even as a vegetable dip.

125 ml slivered almonds

1 small jar roasted red peppers, drained

1 free-range egg yolk

2 large cloves garlic, sliced

2.5 ml finely grated orange rind

Sea salt and freshly milled black pepper

125 ml extra virgin olive oil

60 ml orange juice

15 ml sherry vinegar or red wine vinegar

Toss the almonds in a dry pan over medium heat for 2–3 minutes until golden brown. Set aside and allow to cool.

In the bowl of a blender, place the almonds, roasted red peppers, egg yolk, garlic and orange rind, and season with sea salt and freshly milled black pepper. Blend for a short while until it reaches a paste consistency.

Set the blender on a low speed and slowly pour in the olive oil, much like you would if making a mayonnaise. When you have poured in about half of the oil, add the orange juice and your chosen vinegar. Slowly add the remaining oil while continuing to blend until it forms an emulsion.

Retaste to check for seasoning.

The sauce will keep in the refrigerator for up to five days.

Makes about 275 ml

Christine Stevens' Carrot Top, Coriander and Almond Pesto

When she and we lived in Cape Town, Christine used to supply our restaurant with lovely, fresh vegetables. I will never forget her bright-green tender broad beans, and I think of her every time they are in season. Christine is a professional garden designer – she creates and manages vegetable and herb gardens for hotels and restaurants – and cookbook author.

She says: 'I love to find ways to use all parts of the vegetables we grow. So much is thrown away, and a lot of fresh food that is discarded is so very good to eat. This very tasty carrot top pesto is a firm favourite in our family – so simple to make, no actual cooking, just a bit of chopping. The main ingredient is the feathery green carrot tops so often tossed out or thrown onto the compost heap. The pesto is delicious spooned over a bowl of roasted carrots, but also equally good mixed into a bowl of pasta or quinoa for a quick and healthy supper.
I also often use it as a salad dressing.'

250 ml chopped green carrot tops (preferably the smaller ones; they have a sweeter taste)

125 ml chopped fresh coriander

125 ml chopped almonds

15 ml chopped capers

Grated rind of ½ lemon

1 clove garlic, crushed

Extra virgin olive oil

Place the chopped ingredients, lemon rind and crushed garlic into a jar and pour over some olive oil. Stir until you have a pesto consistency. You don't really need to season this pesto as the capers add a good salty kick.

Keep it in a jar out of the refrigerator in a cool place and it will last for up to three days.

Makes about 500 ml

COOK'S NOTE

Chop the ingredients as fine as you like. I tend to do a fine chop, but if time is short I just blitz everything in a NutriBullet.

Colly's Stick Blender Mayonnaise

This method has been around for quite a while, but I didn't know about it until my friend Colly told me! This is my version. I prefer for my mayo to use half olive oil and half a lighter oil like sunflower, peanut or grapeseed. At the moment I am going through a phase where I like apple cider vinegar. Don't use balsamic or red wine vinegar as it will colour the mayo.

1 stick blender and the tall glass jar that comes with it.

Put the following into the glass jar, in this order:

- 2 free-range egg yolks (better if they are at room temperature, and no problem if some egg white drops into the jar)
- 190 ml sunflower, peanut or grapeseed oil
- 180 ml extra virgin olive oil
- 15 ml lemon or lime juice
- 5 ml apple cider, rice or white wine vinegar
- 7.5 ml Dijon mustard
- Sea salt and freshly milled black pepper
- 15 ml honey, moskonfyt or agave nectar
- 2 fat cloves garlic, chopped (optional, unless you want a garlicky mayo)

Before switching it on, gently insert the blender through the oil to the bottom of the jar. Switch on the blender and immediately the egg will start emulsifying with the oil. Pull the blender slowly upwards through the oil and the mayonnaise will make itself on the way up.

If the mayonnaise is too thick, you can add some hot water to thin it down.

Makes slightly more than 375 ml

Homemade Garam Masala

There is curry powder off the shelf, and then there is homemade garam masala. When I was cooking on *Expresso*, I had a dish to prepare and I thought it would be quite fun to make my own garam masala. This is the result.

10 ml cumin seeds

10 ml coriander seeds

10 ml fenugreek seeds

10 ml yellow mustard seeds

2.5 ml cardamom seeds (open the green pods and take out the little black seeds)

10 ml white peppercorns

10 ml whole cloves

5 ml hot chilli powder

10 ml turmeric

2.5 ml ground cinnamon

Toss all the seeds, the peppercorns and cloves in a dry frying pan over medium heat to toast them for a few seconds and to release the aromas. Allow to cool and then grind to a fine powder in a coffee grinder or using a pestle and mortar.

Transfer to a small bowl and add the chilli powder, turmeric and cinnamon.

Stir well and store in an airtight container.

Makes about 80 ml

Nina Timm's
All-Purpose Spice Mix

Nina says: 'I make a batch of this spice mix almost once a month. I use it for roast leg of lamb, chops, meatballs and, of course, lamb ribs. The secret to the mix is in dry-roasting the spices. It releases the oils and intensifies the flavour. This all-purpose spice mix also does not require any rocket science or fancy ingredients, but three or four basic ingredients that I want to bet you have in your spice rack. If not, you should get them; it is so worth it.'

Here are my basic spice ingredients:

Salt: I prefer using a coarse salt, because it serves as an abrasive when grinding the other spices.

Pepper: Black pepper is my preferred variety for this mix. Although we simply describe peppercorns as pepper, did you know that black pepper is the cooked and dried unripe fruit, green pepper is the dried unripe fruit, while white pepper is the ripe fruit seeds?

Coriander: Coriander is an annual herb that you should have in your garden. It grows so quickly and without much effort. All parts of the plant are edible, but the fresh leaves and the dried seeds are the parts most used in cooking. In South Africa, it's often referred to as the 'biltong spice' or the 'meat spice', because traditionally biltong (jerky) is made with coriander. To get the maximum flavour from coriander seeds, you need to dry-fry them (see below for how to do this). They can then be used whole or crushed.

Herbs: For my all-purpose meat spice, I prefer rosemary or thyme. Rosemary can take over a little, so use her sparingly. One or two small twigs are more than enough.

250 ml coriander seeds
60 ml black peppercorns
125 ml coarse sea salt
2–3 sprigs fresh rosemary or thyme

Heat a pan or skillet (no oil), add the coriander seeds and dry-fry them over medium heat while stirring continuously. When you get their unique aroma, they are ready. Remove from the skillet and cool.

Place the coriander seeds and the rest of the ingredients into a spice grinder, pestle and mortar or even a coffee grinder. Process to the desired texture. I prefer a coarser texture.

Keep in an airtight container until needed.

Makes about 500 ml

Zola Nene's uJeqe, a Traditional Steamed Bread

I was so fortunate to work with Zola Nene on *Expresso* for three years. I have basked in the reflected glory of her subsequent success. She is a modern technology lady and uses all manner of social media to share her recipes. When I asked her for one of her recipes, she sent me this one for traditional steamed bread.

4 x 250 ml cake flour

10 g instant dry yeast

15 ml white sugar

5 ml sea salt

625 ml warm water

Place the flour, yeast, sugar and salt into a bowl and mix together.

Slowly add the water, a little at a time, and mix until a soft dough forms (you may need more or less water).

Tip the dough onto a floured surface and knead for about 10 minutes until it is smooth and elastic.

Place the dough into a greased bowl, cover with plastic wrap and allow to prove for 30 minutes or until doubled in size.

Tip out again onto a floured surface and knead to knock out the air. Form into a ball and place into a heatproof dish. Cover with plastic wrap and leave to rise again until doubled in size.

Set the dish into a saucepan filled with boiling water that reaches halfway up the sides of the dish. Cover with a lid and simmer for 1½–2 hours or until the uJeqe is cooked through and springs back to the touch. Top up the saucepan with water, if necessary, during steaming.

Makes 1 loaf

Recipe Index

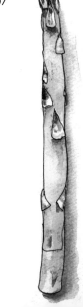